Folens
AGES 7–9

✓ *Accessing...*

HISTORY 4

Rhona Whiteford

Acknowledgements

Historic Royal Palaces/newsteam.co.uk, pg40b; An Allegory of the Tudor Succession: The Family of Henry VIII, c.1589-95 (oil on panel) by English School (16th century), Yale Center for British Art, Paul Mellon Collection, USA/Bridgeman Art Library, pg46; Archivo Iconografico, S.A./CORBIS, pg 11 (top); Bettmann/CORBIS, pp. 19 (bottom), 20 (bottom), 23, 33; Bojan Brecelj/CORBIS, pg 15; by permission of the Syndics of Cambridge University Library, pg 41; The British Museum pp. 5, 6 (top), 6 (bottom); CORBIS, pp. 16, 17; Corel, pp. 12 (top), 12 (bottom), 14 (top); David Muench/CORBIS, pg 29; David Turnley/CORBIS, pg 27 (bottom); Gianni Dagli Orti/CORBIS, pg 48; Historical Picture Archive/CORBIS, pg 40 (top); Howard Davies/CORBIS, pg 27 (top); Hulton-Deutsch Collection/CORBIS, pp. 18 (bottom), 20 (top), 22, 24, 28; James Strachan/Getty Images, pg 4; Kevin Schafer/CORBIS, pg 35 (top); Keystone/Getty Images, pg 19 (top); Ludovic Maisant/CORBIS, pg 31 (top); Manx National Heritage, pg 38; Meeting at the Field of the Cloth of Gold, 7th June 1520, after Hans Holbein the Elder (1460/5-1524) (oil on canvas) by Friedrich Bouterwek (1806-67) Chateau de Versailles, France/Bridgeman Art Library: Lauros/Giraudon/Bridgeman Art Library, pg 44; National Portrait Gallery, London, pg 42; R Sheridan/Ancient Art & Architecture Collection, pp. 7 (top), 7 (bottom), 8, 11 (bottom); Ted Spiegel/CORBIS, pg 30; The Mary Rose Trust, pg. 47 (top), 47 (bottom); The Robert Opie Collection, pg 21; Tim Page/CORBIS, pg 26 (top); Tim Rooke/Rex Features, pg 26; Topham Picturepoint, pg 18 (top); Werner Forman/CORBIS, pp. 34 (top), 34 (bottom), 35 (bottom), 37; With kind permission of Associated Newspapers, pg 25; Zone/Alamy, pg 13

© 2005 Folens Limited, on behalf of the author.
United Kingdom: Folens Publishers, Apex Business Centre, Boscombe Road, Dunstable, LU5 4RL.
Email: folens@folens.com

Ireland: Folens Publishers, Greenhills Road, Tallaght, Dublin 24.
Email: info@folens.ie

Poland: JUKA, ul. Renesansowa 38, Warsaw 01-905.

Commissioning editor: Zoë Nichols
Editor: Melody Ismail
Layout artist: Patricia Hollingsworth
Illustrations: James Field (SGA Illustration)
Cover design: Philippa Jarvis
Cover image: Gianni Dagli Orti/CORBIS

First published 2005 by Folens Limited.

British Library Cataloguing in Publication Data. A catalogue record for this publication is available from the British Library.

ISBN 1 84303 675 4

Contents

© Folens

The River Nile

An Egyptian mummy

Soul houses

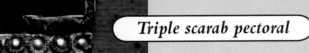

Triple scarab pectoral

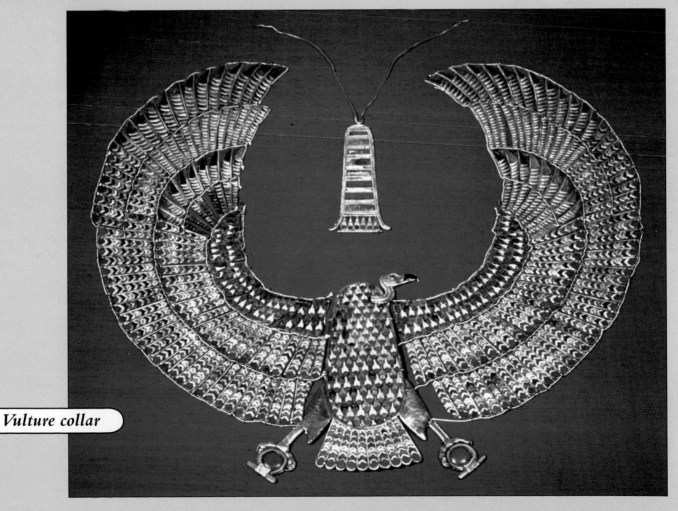

Vulture collar

Hunting on the Nile

Wealthy Egyptians

Agricultural landscape

Agricultural activity

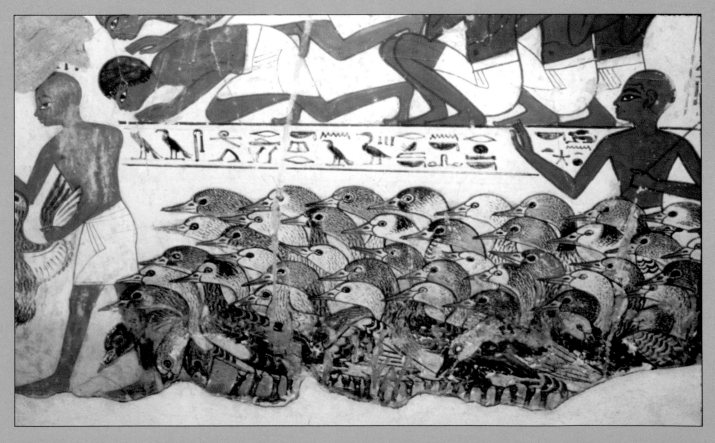

Queen Hatshepsut's Mortuary Temple

The pyramids, Giza

A workers' village

Temple of Ramesses II

Hieroglyphic writing

German tanks in France

Fire fighting during the Blitz

Seaside holiday

Bombed home

Building an Anderson shelter

Londoners sleeping in an underground station

Evacuee children

Children wearing gas masks

         © Folens

Wartime foods

Air raid warden

A Jewish family wearing the Star of David

Wartime schooling

Text on blackboard:

WHAT DO WE MEAN BY 1 HITLERISM. 2. DEMOCRACY?

Hitlerism is a form of government controlled by one man's will.

Democracy is a form of government controlled by Parliament and the majority of the people.

I SMELL PINEAPPLE

Daily Mail
NO. 15.290 ONE PENNY FOR KING AND EMPIRE TUESDAY, MAY 8, 1945

TUESday FIELD-DAY

3-POWER ANNOUNCEMENT TO-DAY; BUT BRITAIN KNEW LAST NIGHT

VE-DAY—IT'S ALL OVER

All quiet till 9 p.m.—then the London crowds went mad in the West End

THE Face of Victory—by day and night: Roadways in and around Piccadilly circus were jammed nearly solid yesterday afternoon by crowds waiting to hear VE-Day announced. Then they decided not to wait—they began to celebrate. These Daily Mail pictures give you a vivid impression of the great concourse of joy—above by day; on the left, by night. Other scenes—Pages THREE and FOUR.

PM put off the big speech

UNTIL TO-DAY

By WILSON BROADBENT, Diplomatic Correspondent

GERMANY surrendered unconditionally to the Allies yesterday. But there will be no official announcement of victory until 3 p.m. to-day—officially described as VE-Day—when Mr. Churchill will give the news to the world.

He will follow this with an address to the House of Commons, and at 9 p.m. the King will speak to Britain and the Empire.

Mr. Churchill's private room at the House of Commons was last night "wired-up" so that if he wishes he can make a broadcast from there.

To-day's announcement will be made simultaneously in London, Washington, and Moscow. To-day, therefore, is the first of the promised two-days V-holiday for the country.

Broadcasts will also be made by General Eisenhower and Field-Marshals Montgomery and Alexander.

Mr. Churchill's two statements to-day will not affect his intention to broadcast at length on Thursday night, the fifth anniversary of his assumption of the Premiership.

After his statement in the House of Commons, Mr Churchill will propose the adjournment of business while M.P.s attend a special Service of Thanksgiving at St. Margaret's Church, Westminster. They will then return to the House of Commons, adjourn, and arrange to meet again on Wednesday.

Until shortly before 8 o'clock last night it was fully expected that Mr. Churchill would be able to announce the news that the war was over.

Victory lunch

He had been standing by the microphone from some time after 7 o'clock, and everything was ready for him to break into the normal programmes of the B.B.C.

Earlier in the day he had been speaking on the Transatlantic telephone to Washington, and he also had several calls to Moscow. His object was to obtain an agreed time for releasing the big news.

There had been a previous agreement that there should be simultaneous times for release. Apparently in London it was understood that Monday would be suitable to all concerned.

In anticipation of this important occasion Mr Churchill gave a special Victory luncheon party at No. 10, Downing-street for the Chiefs of Staff, whose health he personally proposed.

After luncheon Mr. Churchill was ready to broadcast, but no news of Washington's or Moscow's assent had been received.

It was nearly 6 o'clock when it was learned that both the United States and the Soviet Government were in favour of postponing the formal announcing until this afternoon.

Moscow preferred this course because of certain final formalities connected with the German surrender, which will take place to-day. Washington had other reasons which are not yet known. So Mr. Churchill, finding himself in a minority, had to agree.

CZECHS TOLD TO 'SMASH GERMANS'

Czech-controlled radio early to-day appealed to Patriots on the barricades to attack and smash German positions. Radio declared that "Protector" Frank yesterday made "arrogant" offer to resign and order cease fire if Czechs would leave barricades.—Reuter.

TARAKAN NEARLY CUT IN TWO

Manila, Tuesday.—Allies cleared ground east of the main oilfield on Tarakan, off Borneo, and advanced across the island to within a mile and a half of the east shore. Fighting continues for Tarakan town.—B.U.P.

4

U.S. made it VE-Day all the same

Work walk-out

From DON IDDON, Daily Mail Correspondent

NEW YORK, Monday.

THIS was VE-Day in the U.S.—official or not.

The celebrations began in New York at breakfast-time, a few minutes after word came from Rheims, France, that Germany had surrendered unconditionally to Britain, the United States, and Russia.

They went on all day despite an avalanche of confused messages, lack of official confirmation, half-denials, and a barrage of rumours that the surrender was a hoax.

The American public, and particularly the New York public, this time was determined that this was the end of the war in Europe, and resolved to commemorate it.

The first reaction, and it was the same all over Manhattan, was to jab open windows, tear up telephone directories, and hurl paper into the streets.

For hours tons upon tons of ticker tape, torn-up newspapers, envelopes, letters, magazines, and in some instances hats and waste-paper baskets, cascaded down.

Jammed roads

Tens of thousands of people abandoned work and rushed into the Times-square area, shouting and singing. Motorists blew their hooters, factory whistles shrieked, and in New York Bay ships sounded their sirens.

Bands of Service men and girls paraded the avenues, waving flags, shouting and yelling, planting kisses on strangers, cavorting in and out of bars.

Great stores, offices, the banks, the factories closed down as staffs walked out *en masse*.

Traffic was completely tied up in mid-town as throngs of gesticulating, laughing people jammed roadways, jumped on to the running-boards of private cars, taxis, and buses.

At first city officials, led by Mayor La Guardia, attempted to curb the jubilation.

Over the radio came a reminder that there was nothing official, that it was merely a report which had declared that war in Europe was over. The people ignored the advice

Daily Mail

IN accordance with the expressed desire of the Government that workers generally should enjoy a day's holiday following the announcement of the cessation of hostilities in Europe, The Daily Mail, in common with other London morning newspapers, will not be published on Thursday.

SYMBOL of the mood of London, this man, at the top of a lamp-post, waves a flag above the crowds.—Daily Mail picture.

The war still goes on here—

PRAGUE BOMBED AS SS SHOOT CZECH CIVILIANS

GERMAN bombs are falling on Prague for the first time as the war in Europe enters its last hours. In defiance of surrender orders, German forces in Czecho-Slovakia are fighting on. They are venting their last spite on the Czechs, shooting them down ruthlessly in the streets of the capital.

Refugees from Prague who have reached Allied-occupied Pilsen say that, in many cases, the S.S. went through the city driving people out of their houses into the streets.

And there other S.S. men mowed them down with machine-guns. The S.S., according to the refugees, know they will probably be executed when caught and have abandoned all normal conduct.

That the S.S are completely out of hand is indicated in a broadcast by the German commander in Bohemia and Moravia warning his troops to respect international law.

Two columns of General Patton's tanks are racing to Prague's rescue and were last reported seven miles south of the capital.

A Czech Spitfire squadron and formations of large aircraft carrying Czech ground troops, have left Britain for Czecho-Slovakia.

Broadcasting from London last night, Dr. Hubert Ripka, Czecho-Slovak Minister of Foreign Trade, said that, by fighting on after the general capitulation, the Germans had placed themselves beyond the law and would be dealt with as saboteurs.

Pilsen kisses

PILSEN, Monday.

LIEUT.-GENERAL MAJEWLSKI, commanding the German gar-

BACK PAGE—Col. EIGHT

Beacon chain begun by Piccadilly's bonfires

By GUY RAMSEY

LONDON, dead from six until nine, suddenly broke into victory life last night. Suddenly, spontaneously, deliriously. The people of London, denied VE-Day officially, held their own jubilation. "VE-Day may be to-morrow," they said, "but the war is over to-night." Bonfires blazed from Piccadilly to Wapping.

The sky once lit by the glare of the blitz shone red with the Victory glow. The last trains departed from the West End unregarded. The pent-up spirits of the throng, the polyglot throng that is London in war-time, burst out, and by 11 o'clock the capital was ablaze with enthusiasm.

Processions formed up out of nowhere, disintegrating for no reason, to re-form somewhere else. Waving flags, marching in step, with linked arms or half-embraced, the people strode down the great thoroughfares—Piccadilly, Regent-street, the Mall, to the portals of Buckingham Palace.

They marched and counter-marched so as not to get too far from the centre. And from them, in harmony and discord, rose song. The songs of the last war, the songs of a century ago. The songs of the beginning of this war—"Roll out the Barrel" and "Tipperary"; "Ilkla Moor" and "Loch Lomond"; "Bless 'em All" and "Pack Up Your Troubles."

ROCKETS AND SONGS

Rockets—found no-one knows where, set-off by no-one knows whom—streaked into the sky, exploding not in death but a burst of scarlet fire. A pile of straw filled with thunder-flashes salvaged from some military dump spurted and exploded near Leicester-square.

Every car that challenged the milling, moiling throng was submerged in humanity. They climbed on the running-boards, on the bonnet, on the roof. They hammered on the panels. They shouted and sang.

Against the drumming on metal came the clash of cymbals, improvised out of dustbin lids. The dustbin itself was a football for an impromptu Rugger scrum. Bubbling, exploding with gaiety, the people "mafficked." Headlights silhouetted couples kissing, couples cheering, couples waving flags.

Every cornice, every lamp-post was scaled. Americans marched with A.T.S., girls in civvies, fresh from their work benches, ran by the side of battle-dressed

Continued in Back Page, Col. 6

SCHACHT SAVED BY 'FIFTH'

Niemoller, too

Daily Mail Special Correspondent

ALLIED H.Q., Italy, Monday.

SOME of the most famous victims of Nazi-ism have been rescued by the Fifth Army from the Prager Wildsee prison camp, near Obbiaco, Italy.

Among them was **Pastor Niemoller**, head of the German Confessional Church, whose defiance of Hitler led to a seven years' incarceration in concentration camps.

A few hours after his release Pastor Niemoller held a service in the lounge of a hotel.

His text was the words of Isaiah:

For the mountains shall depart, and the hills be removed; but my kindness shall not depart from thee, neither shall the covenant of my peace be removed, saith the Lord that hath mercy on thee.

In all, the Fifth Army saved 126 hostages, including **Dr. Schuschnigg**, former Chancellor of Austria who during the week-end was erroneously reported to have been executed.

Dr. Schuschnigg's wife was also found. **M. Leon Blum**, former Socialist Premier of France, and his wife, were also freed.

'Evil Hitler'

The camp in which these famous people were found was a smallish affair—a group of huts around a chateau on a hillside. But behind its barbed wire the Fifth Army men found many high officers—Greek, Russian, Hungarian—and a number of Germans including **Dr. Schacht**, former German Minister of Finance and President of the Reichsbank.

Asked if Hitler was sane, Dr. Schacht said: "In some things no, in others he is a genius."

Someone suggested an evil genius, and Schacht said: "Yes, an evil genius . . . an evil and diabolical genius."

VE-WEATHER

Strait of Dover yesterday: Victory weather, with hours of sunshine. Day temperature, 69deg.

GOEBBELS' BODY IN A SHELTER

GOEBBELS, the German Propaganda Minister, his wife, and five children have been found dead in Berlin.

Moscow says that their bodies were found in an air-raid shelter near the Reichstag, and it has been established that all died of poisoning.

No trace has been found of the bodies of Hitler or Goring.

There was speculation in London last night whether the Nazi leaders may have fled to a place of hiding.

It was pointed out, however, that their bodies may have been destroyed in the wreckage of the burning Chancellery or some other building.

Moscow radio last night reported, says *B.U.P.*, that troops had penetrated deep into an underground fortress in the basement of Hitler's Chancellery.

"Smoke is pouring from an unexplored depth into which we had been unable to penetrate," said the radio.

MONTY MEETS ROKOSSOVSKY

4 toasts at lunch

TWENTY-FIRST ARMY GROUP, Monday.—Field-Marshal Montgomery lunched to-day with Marshal Konstantin Rokossovsky at Wismar.

Toasts were drunk to the Allied armies, Mr Churchill, Marshal Stalin, and President Truman.—*Reuter.*

Home by searchlight

There will be a searchlight display by the A.A. over Central London and London suburbs on VE-Night, from 11.45 p.m. to 12.15 a.m. and again on the next night at the same time.

ARRESTED POLES MAY BE TRIED BY LUBLIN

LUBLIN radio said yesterday that the Polish Provisional Government may demand that General Okulicki and others of the 16 Poles arrested by the Russians be tried both in Warsaw and Moscow for high treason.

The radio said: "Public opinion in Poland has received with indignation the news of the action of Okulicki and his accomplices, who are accused of carrying out diversionary activities against the Red Army.

"Because the criminal activities of Okulicki and his accomplices were also directed against the reborn Polish State, it constitutes high treason.

"The Provisional Government reserves the right to demand that Okulicki and his accomplices be turned over to the Polish authorities to be indicted in the courts of the Republic as well."

M. Mikolajczyk, former Polish Prime Minister in London, announced yesterday that he is preparing a statement on the arrests.

He said that the arrested men cannot be accused of diversionary acts against the Soviet forces, as they were sincere partisans of a Polish-Soviet understanding.

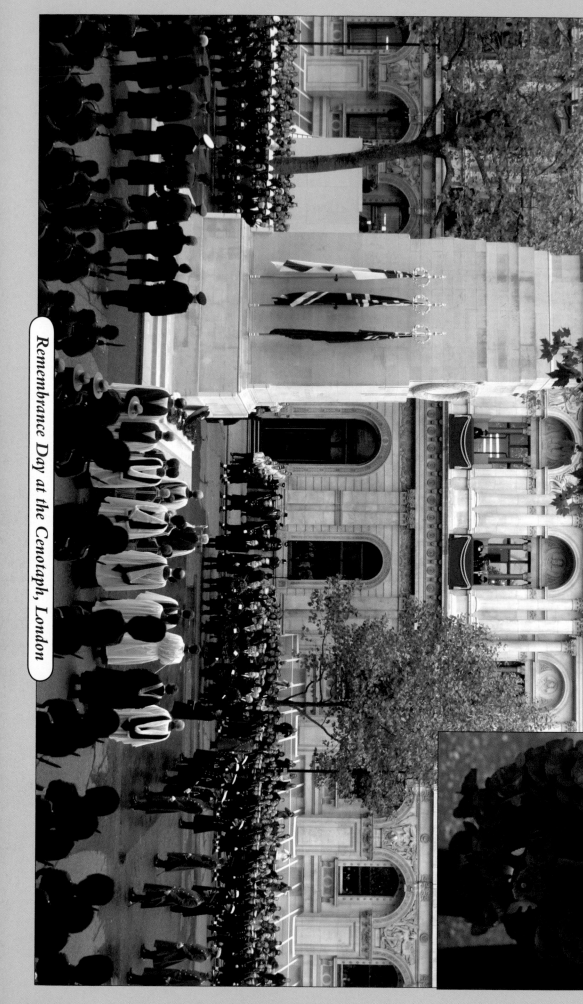

Remembrance Day at the Cenotaph, London

Afghan children at refugee camp, Pakistan

UN armoured transport, Bosnia

Viking longship

© Folens

Typical fjord terrain

The Lindisfarne Stone

A Viking longhouse

Viking farmstead

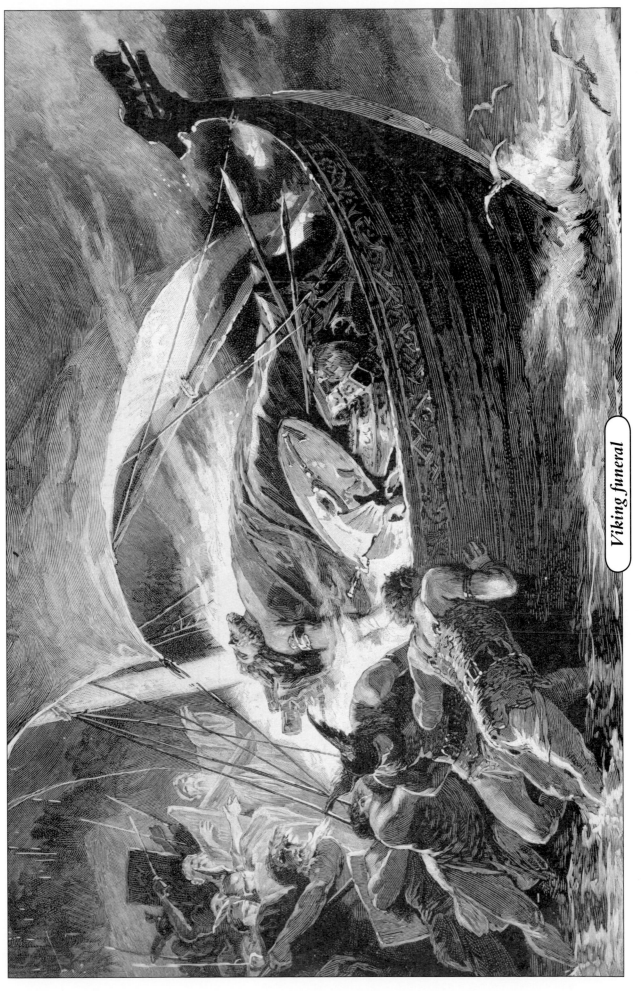

Viking funeral

Viking smiths working

Viking artefacts

Viking runes

Gunnar in the snake-pit

Viking jewellery

An illustrated manuscript

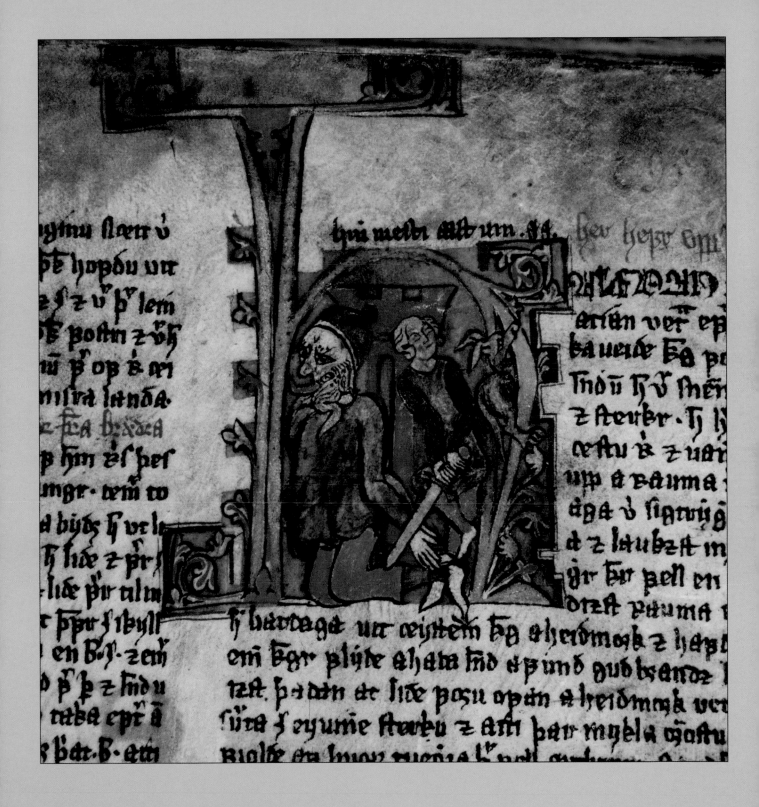

Thorwald's Cross-Slab

The Althing

Hampton Court interior, 1838

Hampton Court today

The coronation of Henry VIII

King Henry VIII, 1520

Henry's six wives

Catherine of Aragon

Anne Boleyn

Jane Seymour

Anne of Cleves

Catherine Howard

Catherine Parr

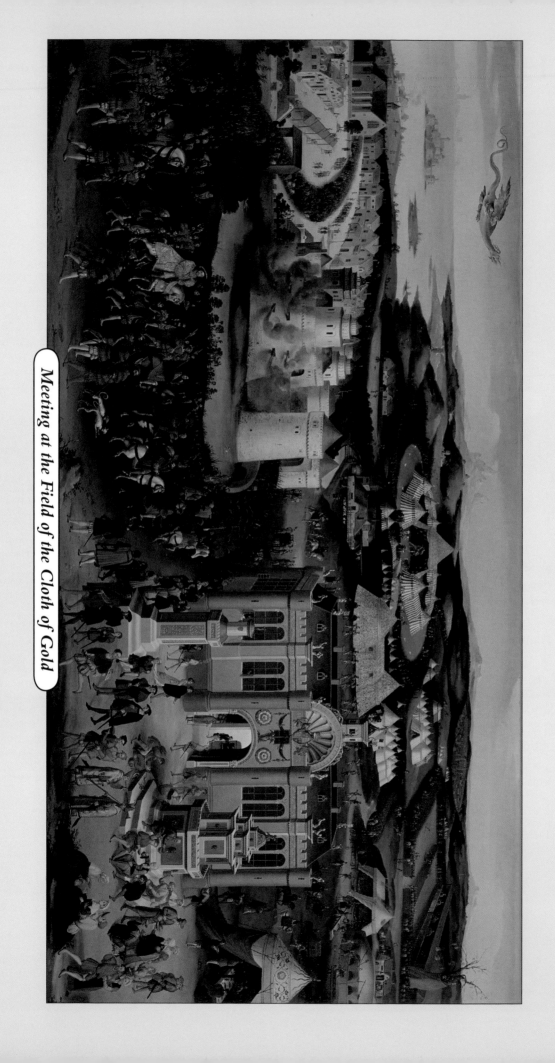

Meeting at the Field of the Cloth of Gold

Henry VIII's pastimes

Dancing

Hawking

Reading

Jousting

The family of Henry VIII

46 © Folens

The Mary Rose

ANNO · ETATIS ·   · SVÆ · XLIX ·

King Henry VIII, 1540

TAKE TEN YEARS

1990s

Published by Evans Brothers Limited
2A Portman Mansions
Chiltern Street
London W1U 6NR

First published in 2001
First published in paperback in 2003

Printed in Spain by GRAFO, S.A. – Bilbao

British Cataloguing in Publication Data

Ross, Stewart
   1990s. - (Take ten years)
   1.Nineteen nineties - Juvenile literature 2.History, modern
   - 20th century - Juvenile literature
   I.Title II.Nineteen nineties
   909.8'29

ISBN 0237525704

Acknowledgements

Editor: Nicola Edwards
Design: Tinstar Design
Production: Jenny Mulvanny

cover (top left, bottom centre and bottom right) Rex Features (top right, centre left, centre, centre right, bottom left Topham Picturepoint
page 4 (from top to bottom) Mandela Associated Press/Topham, Topham, Associated Press/Topham, Associated Press/Topham, Topham Picture Point page 5 (from top to bottom) David Hartley/Rex Features, Jeremy. S. Hibbert/Rex Features, Topham Picture Point, Rex Features page 8 Associated Press/Topham page 9 (top) Associated Press/Topham (bottom) UNEP/P Gleizes/Topham page 10 (top) Chesnot/Rex Features (bottom) Topham Picture Point page 11 (left) Associated Press/Topham (right) Associated Press/Topham page 12 (top left) Associated Press/Topham (top right) Topham Picture Point (bottom) Associated Press/Topham page 13 (middle right) Topham Picture Point (bottom) Topham Picture Point page 14 Topham Picture Point page 15 (left) Associated Press/Topham (right) Associated Press/Topham page 16 (top) Associated Press/Topham (bottom) Associated Press/Topham page 17 (top) Rex Features (bottom) Nils Jorgensen/Rex Features page 18 Charles Sykes/Rex Features page 19 Rex Features page 20 Villard/Rex Features page 21 (top) Jon Bradley/Rex Features (bottom left) Rex Features (bottom right) Topham Picture Point page 22 (top) Associated Press/Topham (bottom) Press Association/Topham page 23 (top) Associated Press/Topham (bottom) Associated Press/Topham page 24 Topham Picture Point page 25 (top) Associated Press/Topham (middle) Gabriel Piko/Sipa Press/Rex Features (bottom) Rex Features page 26 (left) Iwasa/Rex Features (right) Rex Features page 27 (top) Topham Picture Point (bottom) Rex Features page 28 (left) Rex Features (right) Rex Features page 29 (top) Rex Features (middle) Rex Features (bottom) Adrian Brooks/Rex Features page 30 (top) Associated Press/Topham (bottom) David Hartley/Rex Features page 31 (top) Associated Press/Topham (bottom) James Morgan/Rex Features page 32 Rex Features page 33 (top) Jeremy. S. Hibbert/Rex Features (bottom) Jorgensen/Rooke/Rex Features page 34 (top) Rex Features page 35 (top) Topham Picture Point (bottom) Sipa/Rex Features page 36 (left) Topham PicturePoint (right) Associated Press/Topham page 37 (top) Rex Features (bottom) Rex Features page 38 (centre right) Rex Features (bottom left) Topham Picture Point page 39 Rex Features page 40 (top) Sipa/Rex Features (bottom) Rex Features page 41 Sipa/Rex Features page 42 (top) Martin Cleaver/Topham Picture Point (bottom left) John M Mantel/Rex Features (bottom right) Topham Picture Point page 43 (top) Erik Pendzich/Rex Features (bottom) Melde Press/Rex Features page 44 (from the top) Associated Press/Topham, Topham Picture Point, Rex Features, Topham Picture Point, Topham Picture Point page 45 (From the top) Brad Rickerby/Rex Features, Topham Picture Point, Rex Features, Rex Features, Kevin Kolczynski/Rex Features.

TAKE TEN YEARS
1990s

STEWART ROSS

EVANS BROTHERS LIMITED

Contents

1996 The IRA detonates a bomb in London's Docklands, ending its cease-fire. Sixteen Dunblane primary school children and their teacher are murdered by a lone gunman. A bomb explosion rocks the Olympic Games in Atlanta, Georgia. Prince Charles and Diana, Princess of Wales, are divorced. Bill Clinton is re-elected US President.

1997 Deng Xioaping dies in Beijing. An adult mammal, 'Dolly the sheep', is cloned for the first time. New Labour wins a landslide victory in the British General Election. There are unprecedented displays of public mourning throughout the world following the death of Diana, Princess of Wales, in a Paris car crash. Britain hands Hong Kong back to China. The economies of Eastern Asia slip into deep recession. Mother Teresa of Calcutta dies.

1998 An ice storm wreaks havoc in Canada. The 'Good Friday Agreement' signals success in the Northern Ireland peace talks. A few months later, a group calling itself the 'Real IRA' explodes a bomb in Omagh, killing 29, in protest against the agreement. The American singer and actor Frank Sinatra dies. The Starr Report into the misdoings of President Clinton is published on the Internet. Hurricane Mitch devastates Central America. The death of former Khmer Rouge dictator Pol Pot is announced. US and British forces bomb Iraq.

1999 A common currency, the Euro, is introduced in the European Union. Scientists discover a link between AIDS in chimpanzees and humans. King Hussein of Jordan dies. President Clinton escapes impeachment. Crisis in Kosovo. A UN peacekeeping force arrives in East Timor. Northern Ireland begins to rule itself again after 25 years of direct rule from London. Giant earthquake rocks Turkey.

The pictures on page 4 show
Nelson Mandela walking free from captivity
Allied planes during Operation Desert Storm
Rioting in Los Angeles
President Mitterrand and Queen Elizabeth II opening the Channel Tunnel rail link
The aftermath of a bomb blast in Oklahoma City

The pictures on page 5 show
Prince Charles and Diana, Princess of Wales
Dolly the Sheep
Mother Teresa
Devastation in the wake of Hurricane Mitch
Earthquake in Turkey

Introduction

The Nineties was a decade of vivid contrasts. Burgeoning peace was scarred by horrific civil conflicts; deep regional recession matched mounting prosperity; spreading democracy and concern for human rights was balanced by ruthless dictatorship and vicious intolerance; the explosion of information and new technology left billions in isolated ignorance; we wept crocodile tears for our ravaged environment but did little to tend it.

The collapse of communism in Eastern Europe and the ending of the Cold War removed the threat of nuclear war. Nevertheless, civil war, notably in Yugoslavia, Rwanda and Afghanistan, brought violence, death and misery to millions. Lives were also lost in keeping the peace, as when the UN force liberated Kuwait from the Iraqis.

The West's economic advance continued apace, but the Russians found managing a free market economy far tougher than expected. And the East Asian boom finally shuddered to a halt to the sound of collapsing banks and businesses from Tokyo to Jakarta. China continued to thrive as the shackles of rigid communist economics were loosened. Though China remained unwilling to embrace democracy, it made encouraging headway elsewhere, most notably in the countries of the former Soviet Union.

Perhaps the greatest threat to democracy and human rights, particularly those of women, was the continued upsurge in militant, fundamentalist Islam. The Iranians softened a little, but not the Taliban of Afghanistan or the terrorists operating in Egypt and Algeria. And even the pro-Western Saudi Arabia refused to allow its ordinary citizens access to the Internet.

As the world became measurably hotter and our climate became more extreme, the environment exercised the minds of governments everywhere. But despite the many conferences, high-sounding resolutions and well-meaning actions of individual states, serious international agreement on how to tackle the problem was not reached. In short, as the human race lurched towards a new millennium, its many causes for optimism were tempered by dark shadows stretching out from its murky past.

YEARS	WORLD AFFAIRS
1990	Namibia becomes independent Germany re-united
1991	START arms limitation treaty signed USSR dissolved
1992	Maastricht Treaty heralds European Union Environmental summit in Rio de Janeiro
1993	Arab–Israeli peace accord signed in Washington DC
1994	Israel and Jordan sign peace deal Free Trade Area of America set up
1995	Widespread protest at French nuclear bomb test in Pacific UN Conference on Women in Beijing demands action on women's rights
1996	Centenary Olympics in Atlanta Global warming confirmed
1997	El Niño disrupts world's weather Massive fires in Indonesia Economic crisis in East Asia Kyoto Earth Summit
1998	Land-for-peace deal over West Bank
1999	European Union starts using a single currency, the Euro

WARS & CIVIL DISORDER	PEOPLE	EVENTS
Iraq invades Kuwait Poll Tax riots in London	Nelson Mandela set free Film star Greta Garbo dies Margaret Thatcher steps down	Hundreds killed in fire during Mecca pilgrimage
United Nations force drives Iraqi forces from Kuwait Civil war looms in Yugoslavia	Tycoon Robert Maxwell found dead in the sea Writer Graham Greene dies Rajiv Gandhi assassinated	Thousands die in Bangladesh floods Hard-line coup fails in Moscow
Riots rock Los Angeles United Nations peacekeeping forces sent to Bosnia Religious disturbances in India US marines sent to help war-torn Somalia	Bill Clinton elected US president Actor and singer Marlene Dietrich dies	Bosnia-Herzegovina declares itself independent of Yugoslavia Czechs and Slovaks vote to split Czechoslovakia
New York's World Trade Center bombed Algeria hit by Muslim terrorists	Sri Lanka's President Premadasa killed by suicide bomber 2-year-old Jamie Bulger killed by two 10-year-old boys Sprinter Ben Johnson is banned from athletics for life for drug taking	Waco siege ends in slaughter Military cancel Nigeria's elections
Civil war intensifies in Afghanistan Genocide in Rwanda IRA calls cease-fire Russia invades Chechnya	Motor racing ace Ayrton Senna killed	Anglican Church ordains women Channel Tunnel opened
Bomb rocks Oklahoma City Massacre of Rwandan Hutu resumed	Prime Minister Rabin shot dead O.J. Simpson found not guilty of murder	Japanese city of Kobe devastated by earthquake
IRA ends cease-fire with bomb in London's Docklands Israel shells UN refugee post in Lebanon	President Bill Clinton re-elected Yasar Kamal sentenced for attacking Turkish government	Lone gunman massacres Scottish schoolchildren Europe bans export of British 'mad cow' beef
Taliban capture Kabul Kaliba seizes power in Zaire	Princess Diana killed in car crash Chinese statesman Deng Xioaping dies Mother Teresa dies	Dolly the sheep cloned New Labour come to power in Britain Hong Kong reverts to China
Riots in Indonesia lead to resignation of President Suharto Serbs massacre civilians in Kosovo Iraq's Saddam Hussein backs down in face of UN threats	President Clinton enmeshed in scandal Singer Frank Sinatra dies	Canada hit by ferocious ice storm Peace deal for Northern Ireland Hurricane Mitch devastates Central America
Russian bombers blast Chechnya UN peacekeeping force arrives in East Timor	President Clinton avoids impeachment King Hussein dies Boris Yeltsin steps down as Russia's President	Northern Ireland begins self rule with coalition cabinet Giant earthquake rocks Turkey

1990

NELSON MANDELA FREE AT LAST

February 11, Cape Town, South Africa   Nelson Mandela today walked free after 27 years in captivity for anti-government activity. 50,000 people assembled outside Cape Town's city hall to welcome him. Mandela, the internationally respected leader of the anti-apartheid African National Congress (ANC), proclaimed, 'I greet you in the name of peace, democracy, and freedom for all.' His words suggest that he will continue to work for the downfall of apartheid and the creation of a multiracial South Africa.

HUBBLE'S SPACE SNAPS

May 20, NASA, USA   A month after being put into orbit round the Earth by the space shuttle *Discovery*, the Hubble telescope has sent back its first image. The picture of a double star 1,260 light years away was captured by a precision-engineered 2.4-metre mirror. It is far clearer than any previously seen picture from outer space. This is possible because light from distant objects reaches the telescope without being distorted by the Earth's atmosphere. NASA scientists hope that the multimillion-dollar Hubble project will add enormously to our understanding of remote corners of the universe.

2,000 loyal supporters greeted the now grey-haired hero as he emerged from the Victor Verster prison with his wife Winnie.

NAMIBIA INDEPENDENT

March 21, Windhoek, Namibia, Southern Africa   In a ceremony attended by dignitaries from almost 150 countries, Namibia, the last colony in Africa, today became an independent nation. Once under German rule, the country broke free from neighbouring South Africa only after a long and bitter conflict and the loss of many hundreds of lives. Namibian President Sam Nujoma has pledged to put the past behind him and strive to uphold democracy and develop closer economic links with South Africa.

1,400 DIE IN MECCA DISASTER

July 2, Mecca, Saudi Arabia The failure of an air-conditioning system today led to the death of over 1,400 Muslim pilgrims in Saudi Arabia. In temperatures of 43°C, some 5,000 Muslim pilgrims crowded into a tunnel linking Mecca's sacred Ka'aba shrine to Mount Arafat. When the air-conditioning failed, panic spread swiftly through the densely packed crowd. In the ensuing stampede almost 1,500 pilgrims were suffocated or crushed to death.

IRAQIS OCCUPY KUWAIT

August 2, Kuwait City Iraq's President Saddam Hussein today surprised most observers by ordering his armed forces into the oil-rich but defenceless Gulf state of Kuwait. Iraqi armour had for some time been massing along Kuwait's frontier, but few believed Saddam would carry out his threat of invasion. The move was immediately condemned by the United Nations. Given the importance of Kuwait's oil reserves and the threat to the even larger oil fields in Saudi Arabia, Iraq's move is bound to be challenged by the United States and its allies.

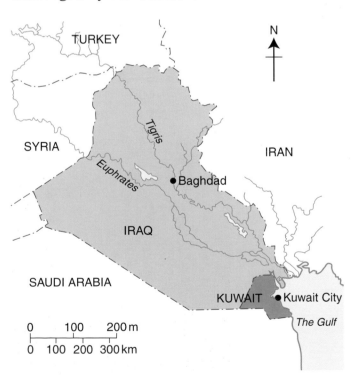

(right) Environmental disaster: a lake of oil flooding from Kuwaiti pipelines severed by Iraqi invaders.

GERMANY RE-UNITED

October 3, Berlin, Germany At midnight the former communist state of East Germany (the German Democratic Republic or GDR) ceased to exist. After 45 years, Germany is once again a single country. German reunification was pushed through by Chancellor Kohl following the collapse of communism in Eastern Europe. It makes Germany by far the most populous European state. Its economic potential is enormous, too. But first the weak economy of the East has to be modernised, a task that even the hard-working and efficient Germans will find difficult.

As midnight struck the huge crowd at Berlin's Brandenberg Gate cheered with delight, and the night sky was lit up with fireworks.

WALESA POLAND'S PREMIER

December 9, Warsaw, Poland Backed by the powerful Roman Catholic Church, Lech Walesa has won an overwhelming 75% of the vote in Poland's presidential election. Ten years ago Walesa was an electrician in his country's communist-run Gdansk shipyard. Defying the authorities, he helped set up Eastern Europe's first independent trade union, Solidarity. The banning of the union and Walesa's arrest made him a hero. Following the collapse of communism, the Nobel Peace Prize winner was an almost automatic choice to lead the new democratic Poland.

Lech Walesa, backed by Solidarity slogans, speaking during his successful campaign for the Polish presidency.

GRETA GARBO DIES

April 15, New York Hollywood film star Greta Garbo died today aged 84. During the 1920s and 30s the beautiful Swedish-born actress won millions of admirers with performances in such block-buster successes as *Anna Karenina* and *Queen Christina*. However, after making her last movie in 1941, Garbo spent the rest of her life living as a recluse.

THATCHER FINALLY GOES

November 22, London Margaret Thatcher has stepped down as Prime Minister of Great Britain. In recent years, 'Maggie' was much criticised for her anti-European policies and her unpopular poll tax. Her leadership was openly challenged because the Conservative party feared she would lose the next general election. She failed to win overall support of her MPs in a party ballot and agreed to stand aside. During her 11-year premiership, 'the Iron Lady' earned a worldwide reputation as a tough opponent of socialism and communism.

NEWS IN BRIEF ...

2.2 MILLION FOR 'MAD COW' RESEARCH

January 9, London The British government today announced £2.2 million for research into bovine spongiform encephalopathy, commonly known as BSE or 'mad cow disease'. The move follows an increase in the number of cases of the disease found in British cattle. There are also fears that eating the meat of diseased cattle may cause a similar brain disease in humans.

MAC-MOSCOW

January 31, Moscow McDonald's, the super-popular American fast food chain, today opened its first outlet in Russia. The Moscow restaurant was thronged, mostly with young people eager to try out the latest Western import. The opening of a McDonald's is yet another sign that Russia is moving fast (too fast, some say) towards a Western-style free market economy.

Defeated: Margaret Thatcher, supported by her husband Dennis, has finally stepped down as Britain's Prime Minister.

1991

DESERT STORM BEGINS

January 17, the Persian Gulf The United Nations, spearheaded by the US, today launched its long-awaited air attack on Iraq. Two days after the expiry of the UN deadline for Iraqi troops to withdraw from Kuwait, Operation Desert Storm hit Baghdad and Iraqi military installations elsewhere with a rain of deadly bombs and missiles. The air assault is preparing the way for ground troops to go in and liberate Kuwait from the forces of the Iraqi dictator, Saddam Hussein.

Allied FKA-18 fighters refuel over Saudi Arabia during Operation Desert Storm.

FLOODS SWEEP BANGLADESH

April 30, Chittagong A tropical cyclone travelling at over 200 kph has brought terrible destruction and loss of life to the coastal regions of Bangladesh. High winds, torrential rain and a tidal wave battered the low-lying area around the port of Chittagong, flattening buildings and sweeping away crops. Vast swathes of the country, one of the poorest in the world, are under water. Perhaps as many as 200,000 people have lost their lives, and the death toll is rising.

Dhaka, capital of Bangladesh, is brought to a standstill by severe flooding.

KUWAIT FREED AT LAST

February 27, Iraq Kuwait, under Iraqi occupation for the last six months, is now free. The UN air assault gave Saddam Hussein's armed forces a terrible battering. In what he called 'the mother of all battles', he lost 150,000 soldiers and countless tanks, guns and aircraft. It now remains to be seen whether he can cling on to power in a defeated, dispirited country.

START'S PEACE DIVIDEND

July 31, Washington DC Today US President Bush and Soviet President Gorbachev signed an epoch-making Strategic Arms Limitation Treaty. Although START began in Geneva in 1982, real progress has been made since the collapse of communist rule in Eastern Europe some 18 months ago. The treaty limits each superpower to 1,600 long-range missile launchers and 6,000 warheads – still enough to destroy civilisation but a significant step towards one day ridding the world of nuclear weapons altogether.

Controversial businessman Robert Maxwell, here flanked by his sons Ian and Kevin.

MYSTERIOUS DEATH OF BRITISH TYCOON

November 5, Tenerife, Canary Islands The naked body of the missing publishing tycoon Robert Maxwell was today found floating in the sea off Tenerife. Maxwell, the flamboyant, Czech-born, self-made multimillionaire, had vanished from his yacht and it was believed he had fallen overboard. Speculation is rife about the precise nature of his death. Even suicide has been suggested, as Maxwell's business empire has recently been going through hard times.

US President George Bush (right) greets Russian Premier Mikhail Gorbachev.

YELTSIN TO THE RESCUE

August 21, Moscow The attempt by hard-line Communists to seize power in the USSR has failed. Two days ago Gennady Yanayev put Soviet President Gorbachev under house arrest, closed radio and TV stations and tried to impose military rule on the USSR. However, Russian President Boris Yeltsin and his supporters refused to be overawed, and barricaded themselves in the Russian parliament building, in Moscow. Faced with the prospect of having to kill fellow citizens, the military backed off. The coup collapsed as swiftly as it had arisen, leaving Yeltsin a Russian national hero.

USSR IS NO MORE

31 December, Moscow The Union of Soviet Socialist Republics, since 1922 the world's leading communist state, today ceased to exist. Born out of civil war and held together by Russian force, the European and Asian states that made up the Union began to go their own ways in the mid-1980s, when President Gorbachev introduced new liberal economic and political reforms. Lithuania, Estonia and Latvia broke away earlier this year. With the resignation of Gorbachev on 25 December, the collapse of Soviet authority was complete.

President Boris Yeltsin rallies his supporters from an unusual vantage point outside the parliamentary offices in Moscow.

NEWS IN BRIEF ...

IRA MORTARS NUMBER 10

February 7, London In one of their boldest moves yet, Irish Republican Army (IRA) terrorists today fired a home-made mortar bomb into the garden of No. 10 Downing Street. The attack on the British Prime Minister's official London residence resulted in broken windows and red faces, but no physical injury. More than one bomb was launched from a specially converted van parked in nearby Whitehall.

GRAHAM GREENE DIES

April 3, Vevey Switzerland Graham Greene, believed by many to be the finest novelist of his generation, died today aged 86. Greene, a convert to Roman Catholicism, wrote such novels as *The Power and the Glory* and *The Heart of the Matter*, about the constant struggle against evil in an imperfect world. Several of his books, such as *Brighton Rock*, were made into successful films.

YELTSIN ELECTED

June 13, Moscow Boris Yeltsin was today chosen as Russia's first freely elected president, although his country has yet to come into independent existence. Now a committed reformer, Yeltsin was once an enthusiastic member of the Communist Party's Central Committee. In capturing 60% of the poll, he overwhelmed backward-looking opposition and set Russia firmly on the road towards democracy and a free market economy.

CIVIL WAR LOOMS IN YUGOSLAVIA

June 27, Ljubljana, Slovenia Yugoslavia, the country set up after the First World War to bring peace and stability to the troubled Balkan region, today seems perilously close to civil war. Slovenia and Croatia have declared themselves independent republics. The Serb-controlled Yugoslav army has begun fighting to bring them to heel. Already many lives have been lost. Given Yugoslavia's profound religious, cultural and ethnic differences, the future is bleak indeed.

FREDDIE MERCURY DIES

November 24, London The music world went into mourning today for the death of the flamboyant 45-year-old singer Freddie Mercury. Best-known as lead singer of the hit UK group Queen, AIDS sufferer Mercury also worked to bridge the gap between popular music and opera. The chart success of 'Barcelona' (1987), with opera singer Monserrat Caballe, was a powerful testimony to his pioneering work.

RAJIV GANDHI ASSASSINATED

May 21, Tamil Nadu, India Prime Minister Rajiv Gandhi was today murdered by a suicide bomber in the south Indian state of Tamil Nadu. The killer was believed to have been a member of a terrorist group fighting for the independence of Tamils in Sri Lanka. Rajiv was the third member of the Gandhi dynasty to lead his country, following in the footsteps of his mother, Indira Gandhi and grandfather, Jawaharlal Nehru.

Rajiv Gandhi, whose brutal assassination has served to draw India even closer into the Tamil struggle to gain control of northern Sri Lanka.

1992

DEATH TOLL MOUNTS IN SOMALIA

January 1, Mogadishu, Somalia The dawn of a new year brings little hope to the people of strife-torn Somalia. Since the fall of President Barre a year ago, their country has become more and more ungovernable. Acting President Ali Mohammed faces not only the powerful Patriotic Front in the south, but a host of aggressive new guerrilla groups. Tens of thousands have already died in the fighting, and even larger numbers of refugees are fleeing to neighbouring Kenya and Ethiopia.

WHITES BACK DE KLERK

March 18, Cape Town, South Africa Nearly 69% of white South Africans voting in yesterday's referendum backed President de Klerk's proposal to give all citizens – black and white – equal political rights. Since coming to power in 1989, de Klerk has moved fast to disband his country's apartheid system. Today's result is a ringing endorsement of his efforts, and ongoing talks with black leaders are now almost certain to lead to South Africa's first multiracial democratic elections. Much remains to be done, however, to bring on board right-wing whites, those of mixed race, and the minority Zulu Inkatha party.

EUROPEAN UNION SET UP

February 7, Maastricht, Netherlands The Maastricht Treaty, hammered out last December after long and tough negotiation, was today signed by the 12 foreign ministers of what is now the European Union. The treaty establishes a single market throughout the Union, starting next year. It also envisages a Union-wide single currency and Central Bank by the end of the decade. However, fearing loss of control over its own affairs, Britain has been given an opt-out on this most controversial issue.

Innocent victims: Somali refugees, driven from their homes in their tens of thousands by the civil war that is tearing their country apart, seek refuge in the neighbouring countries of Kenya and Ethopia.

WAR CLOUDS GATHER OVER BALKANS

March 3, Sarajevo, Bosnia-Herzegovina The perilous situation in the Balkans took a turn for the worse today when Bosnia-Herzegovina declared itself an independent republic. The move is based on the verdict of a referendum, and follows the independence of two other Yugoslav republics, Croatia and Slovenia. However, independence is bitterly opposed by Bosnia-Herzegovina's Serb minority, led by Radovan Karadzic. Supported by the neighbouring Yugoslav province of Serbia, the Bosnian Serbs are unlikely to accept today's move without a fight.

RIOTS ROCK LOS ANGELES

May 1, Los Angeles Riots are today sweeping through the Californian city of Los Angeles. The unrest follows the not-guilty verdict on four policemen accused of beating up black motorist Rodney King. The alleged assault was captured on video, and the city's black community widely expected the police to be found guilty. Disappointment at the verdict led to sporadic violence, which has now escalated into a frenzy of looting, arson and murder. Even firefighters attending blazing buildings have been attacked. At least two dozen deaths and many hundreds of injuries have been reported, and the National Guard has been called in to restore order.

UN TO THE RESCUE

June 30, Sarajevo, Bosnia Canadian troops and armour are today making their way towards Sarajevo, the besieged capital of Bosnia-Herzegovina. Their mission is to open the city's airport so that relief supplies can be flown in for the beleaguered citizens. Sarajevo is currently under siege by Bosnian Serbs led by Radovan Karadzic, who is heavily supported by neighbouring Serbia. The Orthodox Christian Serbs, a minority in the predominantly Muslim state, launched the current bloody civil war when Bosnia-Herzegovina declared itself independent of Yugoslavia in March.

(above) Anarchy in Los Angeles. (right) Families are torn apart as children from Sarajevo are bused to safety.

BOSNIAN ATROCITIES

August 1, Bosnia International observers are increasingly alarmed by reports coming out of Serb-occupied Bosnia. When the Serbs occupy territory formerly held by Muslims and Croats, they implement a policy of 'ethnic cleansing'. In theory, this means encouraging non-Serbs to move out and settle elsewhere. In practice, however, it often means forcible eviction of unwanted peoples from their homes and land. Even more horrifying are harrowing stories of death camps and mass killings. If these turn out to be true – and the Serbs have produced little evidence to prove that they are not – then 'ethnic cleansing' is in fact genocide.

A Serb soldier makes good his escape during Bosnia's bloody civil war.

SLOVAKS VOTE TO STAND ALONE

July 17, Bratislava, Slovakia Slovak deputies today voted to end their state's 74-year marriage with the neighbouring Czechs. Since the 'Velvet Revolution' of 1989, when Czechoslovakia abandoned communism, Slovak nationalism has grown. Following today's decision it seems almost certain to come to fruition with the creation of an independent Republic of Slovakia in the near future.

CLINTON TRIUMPHS IN THE POLLS

November 4, Washington DC Bill Clinton will be the next president of the United States of America. The handsome ex-Governor of Arkansas won 43.2% of the poll, 5% more than his Republican rival George Bush. The race was unusual, however, because a third-party candidate, the Texan business tycoon Ross Perot, captured a remarkable 19%. Clinton, who rose from poor beginnings, has a reputation as a liberal. During his successful election campaign, in which he neatly sidestepped awkward questions about his private life, he called for low taxation and tight controls on government spending.

President-elect: William Jefferson Clinton and his running-mate Al Gore celebrate with their wives their decisive success in the American polls.

RELIGIOUS RIOTS ROCK INDIA

December 7, Bombay, India The army has been called into the city of Bombay today to restore law and order after an outburst of religious rioting that left 41 dead and scores injured. The trouble began in the north of the country, where Hindu fanatics destroyed a 16th-century Muslim mosque in the town of Ayodhya. They claimed the site was needed for a new temple. Their provocative action sparked new displays of India's deep-seated religious unrest, as the news spread and thousands of Muslims and Hindus took to the streets in an orgy of violence.

QUEEN ELIZABETH'S HORRIBLE YEAR

December 25, London In her Christmas message to Britain and the Commonwealth, delivered at 3pm this afternoon, Queen Elizabeth II referred to 1992 as an 'annus horribilis' – a horrible year. The phrase was well chosen. In March, following much press speculation, Prince Andrew and Sarah, Duchess of York, announced their separation. In November, a serious fire ravaged the royal residence of Windsor Castle. And finally, in December, heir to the throne Prince Charles announced that he was separating from his wife, the immensely popular Diana, Princess of Wales. This succession of shocks has led to some suggestions that the British monarchy is in crisis.

Queen Elizabeth II and a firefighter survey the damage to Windsor Castle. The serious fire has brought a disastrous year for the British royals to a wretched conclusion.

NEWS IN BRIEF ...

LI PENG OPENS UP

March 20, Beijing, China The Chinese Prime Minister admitted yesterday that in some areas the traditional communist way was not necessarily the best. In order to compete in world markets, Prime Minister Li Peng told the People's Congress, China should adopt certain aspects of free-market economics. He suggested that limited competition was healthy, and warned workers not to rely on a state-funded job for life, regardless of their performance.

VIVE LA MOUSE!

April 12, Paris Europeans will now no longer have to cross the Atlantic to sample the unique Disney atmosphere. Disneyland Paris, the corporation's latest amusement park, opened today with all the traditional Disney razzmatazz.

BLUE ANGEL DIES

May 6, Paris The German-born actress and cabaret singer Marlene Dietrich died in Paris today aged 90. Once described as 'the most watchable woman in the world', in later life she refused to be photographed.

SUMMIT DISAPPOINTMENT FOR GREENS

June 14, Rio de Janeiro, Brazil The multinational 'Green' summit, which closed today in Rio de Janeiro, left environmentalists bitterly disappointed. Although many grand-sounding treaties to halt global warming and protect the environment were signed, no mechanism was put in place to see that they are upheld. The Green lobby fears that the governments of the world's richer nations will be unwilling to put environmental issues above economic growth.

US MARINES LAND IN SOMALIA

December 9, Mogadishu, Somalia President Bush, backed by UN Secretary-General Boutros Ghali, today sent US marines into Somalia to restore peace and stability to a country ravaged by civil war and famine. At present, most foreign aid ends up in the hands of rival warlords. As the troops rushed ashore, they were met by the lenses and microphones of the world's media; their reception elsewhere in the country will certainly be less friendly.

No expense was spared for the lively opening of Disneyland Paris.

1993

EXPLOSION ROCKS NEW YORK

February 26, New York Shortly after midday a gigantic explosion in an underground car park rocked one of the famous twin towers of Manhattan's World Trade Center. The blast, clearly caused by an enormous bomb, killed five and left a 60-metre-wide smoking crater. Although the main structure of the building remains secure, electrical power was cut and black smoke billowed up the stairways. So far police have no idea who planted the bomb.

It took over six hours to evacuate the 50,000 people who work in the tower, and hundreds were taken to hospital suffering from breathing difficulties.

ISRAEL BOMBARDS LEBANON

July 27, Beirut, Lebanon Today Israel took drastic steps to halt terrorist attacks on her territory. Artillery and aircraft have begun a massive bombardment of the villages in southern Lebanon. It is from here, Israeli sources say, that fanatical Palestinian guerrillas launch rocket attacks on Israeli settlements to the south. Prime Minister Rabin believes his country's show of force will pressure the Lebanese government into taking action against the guerrillas itself. As always in such situations, however, it is civilians who suffer most: the roads to the north are jammed with fleeing refugees.

WACO SIEGE ENDS IN TRAGEDY

A grisly fireball rises above the Waco compound.

April 19, Waco, Texas, USA   At least 74 people died today when US federal agents tried to break into the heavily defended Waco compound of the Branch Davidians cult. The trouble began when agents pierced the surrounding walls and sprayed tear gas inside. Seeing what was happening, leaders of the Christian cult chose to die rather than surrender, and set the compound ablaze. The dead included the cult leader, David Koresh, and 17 children. The Waco siege had begun many weeks earlier, when officers investigating claims of child abuse were refused entry into the compound.

EARTH LOSING ITS OZONE UMBRELLA

March 5, WMO, Geneva, Switzerland   A new report from the World Meteorological Organization feeds growing fears that the Earth's ozone layer is shrinking. The WMO, an agency of the United Nations, reveals that ozone levels over much of Canada and northern Europe have fallen by 20%. The ozone layer acts as a vital filter against the sun's cancer-causing ultraviolet radiation. It is believed that gases known as CFCs, widely used in refrigerators, break down the ozone layer when released into the atmosphere, and many industrial countries have taken steps to stop their production.

YELSTIN CRUSHES OPPOSITION

October 4, Moscow   Government troops today remained loyal to President Yeltsin and obeyed his command to crush a revolt led by Yeltsin's parliamentary opponents. The bitter squabble began in September, when Yeltsin dissolved parliament. Led by the Vice-President Alexander Rutskoy and the Speaker Ruslan Khasbulatov, the assembly responded by remaining in the parliament building and voting to impeach Yeltsin. Rutskoy yesterday brought matters to a head by urging Muscovites to overthrow Yeltsin by force, leaving the president no choice but to send in the army.

HISTORIC AGREEMENT SIGNED IN WASHINGTON

September 13, Washington DC It was a sight most thought they would never see: an Israeli prime minister and a Palestinian leader shaking hands in peace. The occasion was the signing by Prime Minister Yitzhak Rabin and PLO leader Yasser Arafat of a settlement that seeks to end decades of bloodshed. Hammered out through hundreds of hours of tough negotiation, the accord grants a degree of self-government to the Gaza Strip and West Bank, regions conquered by Israel but populated largely by Palestinians. US President Clinton hailed the epoch-making agreement as a 'brave gamble that the future can be better than the past'.

US President Clinton watches as Israeli Prime Minister Yitzhak Rabin and PLO leader Yasser Arafat shake hands in peace.

NIGERIA'S PREMIER GOES BACK ON HIS WORD – AGAIN

June 23, Lagos, Nigeria General Ibrahim Babangida, Nigeria's military leader, has once again made himself the despair of democrats the world over. For the fourth time in the last two-and-a-half years the General promised to restore his country to civilian rule. Presidential elections, certified fair and free by foreign observers, were duly held on June 12. A prominent businessman, Mashood Abiola, was believed to have triumphed. But today General Babangida has declared the elections void, signalling his intention of remaining in power for the foreseeable future.

ALGERIAN GOVERNMENT FIGHTS BACK

November 2, Algiers, North Africa The Algerian government today announced that over the last 48 hours its security forces have tracked down and killed 28 members of the militant Islamic Salvation Front (ISF). Tough government action follows a string of terrorist murders, including that of a former prime minister in August. Over 2,000 have now died in a struggle that began last January, when the army cancelled elections that the fundamentalist and anti-democratic ISF seemed certain to win.

SRI LANKA'S PRESIDENT SLAIN

May 1, Colombo, Sri Lanka Colombo's May Day political rally ended in bloody tragedy today when a suicide bomber took the lives of President Ranasinghe Premadasa and many of his aides and bodyguards. The killer, presumed to have been a supporter of the terrorist Tamil Tigers, had several kilos of high explosive strapped to his body, and detonated them only when he was certain of killing the president. If the assassination is indeed the work of Tamil separatists, then it is the latest act in a long campaign to force the Sri Lankan authorities to grant a Tamil homeland in the north of the country.

NEW HOPE FOR NORTHERN IRELAND

December 15, Downing Street, London Prime Ministers John Major and Albert Reynolds today announced a new peace initiative for Northern Ireland. The Downing Street Declaration accepted the possibility of a united Ireland, but only if agreed by majorities north and south of the border. Elsewhere, the pact stated that a three-month IRA cease-fire would lead to the Republican terrorists being invited to talks on the future of the province.

NEWS IN BRIEF ...

BUSH'S LAST BLAST

January 17, Persian Gulf In one of his last acts as president of the United States, George Bush ordered US warships in the Persian Gulf and Red Sea to send a wave of cruise missiles against targets inside Iraq. Although the Gulf War ended two years ago, Iraq's President Saddam Hussein has yet to comply with United Nations regulations on the manufacture of arms. Bush hopes that this latest attack against Iraq will persuade the obdurate dictator to change his mind.

TODDLER'S KILLERS CHARGED

February 20, Liverpool, England Four days ago the British public were horrified when the battered body of missing two-year-old Jamie Bulger was discovered near a railway embankment. Today their horror is mingled with shock and disbelief as police have charged two 10-year-old boys with the brutal killing. A store security video showing the child-murderers and their victim in a shopping centre gave the police their lead.

CURRENCY CRISIS SWEEPS RUSSIA

July 24, Moscow Russia was thrown into panic today when the government announced that all banknotes made before January 1 1993 will not be valid currency after midnight. The measure, designed to curb inflation and forgery, led to vast crowds besieging banks to demand that their savings be exchanged for legal tender.

MARS OBSERVER GOES MISSING

August 21, Pasadena, California, USA American space scientists today announced that they have lost contact with the space vehicle, Mars Observer. This is a great blow to NASA, as the probe was near the end of its 450-million-mile trip, and was expected soon to be sending back valuable data on the mysterious 'red planet'.

JOHNSON BANNED FOR LIFE

March 5, IAAF, London, England The Canadian sprinter Ben Johnson has been banned from ever taking part in an official race again. The International Amateur Athletic Federation took the decision following a positive drugs test on Johnson. This was the second time the 31-year-old sprinter had been caught cheating. He was previously stripped of his world-record 1988 Olympic 100-metre title because he had used outlawed body-building steroids.

1994

SLAUGHTER IN AFGHANISTAN

January 2, Kabul, Afghanistan The civil war in Afghanistan, raging since the overthrow of President Mohammed Najibullah in 1992, has reached a new pitch of intensity. Over 600 casualties have been reported in recent violence in the capital, Kabul, as rival factions battle to gain the upper hand. Forces loyal to General Dostam have launched an artillery and rocket attack on the city, killing civilians as well as troops loyal to the Muslim coalition of President Rabbani.

Pro-government forces take up positions in the hills above Kabul, defending their capital against the rebel onslaught.

WOMEN ORDAINED AS ANGLICAN PRIESTS

March 12, Bristol, England The ancient cathedral at the heart of Bristol, England, was today the setting for an historic ceremony. In the presence of the archbishops of both Canterbury and York, Bishop Barry Rogerson ordained the Anglican Church's first women priests. By admitting the 32 women to the priesthood, the Church of England brings itself into line with Anglican communions elsewhere, but risks losing some of its most committed followers. Thousands of traditionalists, including over 500 priests, have declared their opposition and said they are considering converting to Roman Catholicism.

A woman priest administers the Anglican communion.

ISRAELI EXTREMIST ON THE RAMPAGE IN WEST BANK

Hebron, West Bank, Occupied Territories, Israel The fragile peace of the West Bank was shattered today when US-born Baruch Goldstein opened fire with an automatic weapon in a crowded Palestinian mosque, killing 29 and wounding dozens more. Goldstein, a right-wing fanatic, was set upon by a crowd of enraged worshippers and beaten to death. News of the massacre spread rapidly throughout Israel, sparking widespread riots and demonstrations. Although acts of mindless slaughter by determined individuals are difficult to prevent, Palestinians were incensed that Israeli security forces had made no move when Goldstein entered the mosque openly carrying his gun.

CHANNEL TUNNEL OPENED

May 6, Calais, France and Folkestone, England The 50-kilometre Channel Tunnel was today officially opened by Queen Elizabeth II and President Mitterand of France. The £10 billion tunnel, one of the great engineering feats of the century, has taken seven years to complete. It will take its first fare-paying passengers at the end of the year. The twin-track rail link, carrying normal trains and a car-carrying shuttle service, means that for millions of travellers arriving in Britain from continental Europe the first glimpse of the 'sceptred isle' will no longer be the celebrated White Cliffs of Dover but a railway marshalling yard outside Folkestone.

Linked at last: President Mitterand and Queen Elizabeth II open the Channel Tunnel rail link.

MILLIONS FLEE RWANDA BLOODBATH

July 4, Kigali, Rwanda Rwanda's bloody civil war is driving millions of refugees to seek shelter in neighbouring Zaire, putting relief agencies there under enormous pressure. The trouble began in April, when President Habyarimana, a Hutu, died in an air crash. The incident sparked an orgy of slaughter between the majority Hutus and their rivals the Tutsi, who make up about 15% of the population. Current estimates suggest that as many as half a million people have died, many brutally slain with axes, spears and clubs, in what is proving to be the most horrific civil conflict of modern times.

IRA OFFER NEW HOPE FOR NORTHERN IRELAND

August 31, Belfast, Northern Ireland Following months of secret negotiation, the Provisional Wing of the terrorist Irish Republican Army (IRA) have called a total cease-fire in their 25-year conflict with the British government. The move reflects a growing realisation that neither side can achieve its aims by force. It is hoped that the gesture will pave the way for peace talks between Republicans, who seek a united, independent Ireland, and Loyalists, who wish Northern Ireland to remain a province of the United Kingdom.

ISRAEL AND JORDAN AT PEACE

October 26, The Israel–Jordan border Another piece in the intricate Middle East peace jigsaw fell into place today when King Hussein of Jordan and Israeli Prime Minister Yitzhak Rabin signed a far-reaching peace treaty. In the presence of US President Bill Clinton, the two leaders ended decades of hostility in a lavish open-air ceremony on their border. In return for peace and security, Israel surrendered 100 square miles of desert and recognised King Hussein's claim to be custodian of Islam's holy shrines in Jerusalem.

RUSSIANS INVADE CHECHNYA

December 11, Chechnya, Russia Powerful Russian forces, including tanks and artillery, today moved into the rebel province of Chechnya. The oil-rich, mostly Muslim region, which has a history of hostility to outside interference, declared itself independent in 1991. Russia refused to accept the break away and, following clear and repeated warnings, Russian President Boris Yeltsin has finally lost patience and ordered in the army. The outgunned Chechnyans are reported to be putting up a stiff resistance.

CHRISTMAS CEASE-FIRE FOR BOSNIA

December 20, Sarajevo, Bosnia It seems that, at last, there may be some progress towards peace in war-torn Bosnia-Herzegovina. Ex-US President Jimmy Carter appears to have brokered a four-month cease-fire between the Bosnian Serbs and their Muslim and Croat foes. It is due to start two days before Christmas. Once the guns have fallen silent, it is hoped negotiations will begin to settle a dispute that has brought untold misery to the shattered Balkan state.

NEW PEACE TREATY FOR ANGOLA

November 20, Lusaka, Zambia For the third time the Angolan government has signed a peace treaty with the National Union for the Total Independence of Angola (UNITA). The pact is intended to end Angola's 19-year civil war, which has cost almost half a million lives. Although UNITA leader Jonas Savimbi failed to show up for the signing in neighbouring Zambia, prompting Angola Premier José dos Santos to decline to sign the agreement personally, hopes are high for its success. The presence of armed UN peacekeepers will help, as will the collapse of South Africa's apartheid regime.

NEWS IN BRIEF ...

EARTHQUAKE ROCKS CALIFORNIA

January 17, Los Angeles, USA Southern California shook with terror as it experienced an earthquake measuring 6.8 on the Richter scale. Centred to the north-west of Los Angeles, the quake brought down buildings and flyovers, and cut services to thousands of homes. At least 50 people are reported dead and many more injured. A curfew has been announced to deter looting in the blacked-out streets and malls.

GRAND PRIX ACE KILLED

May 1, San Marino, Italy The Brazilian racing driver Ayrton Senna was killed today when his car spun and hit a concrete wall at over 100 mph during the San Marino Grand Prix. He had won 41 Grands Prix and was widely regarded as the finest driver on the circuit. His death is bound to lead to calls for tighter safety measures in this most dangerous of sports.

SUPERSTAR CHARGED

June 12, Los Angeles American football superstar O.J. Simpson was today charged with the murder five days ago of his ex-wife Nicole Brown Simpson and her friend Ronald Goldman. The couple were found stabbed to death outside her Los Angeles home. A sporting legend to many Americans, Simpson was arrested after a police car chase that was broadcast live from a TV helicopter. Simpson's popularity and celebrity have meant that the case is already attracting massive media attention.

BRAZIL SAYS THANK YOU

October 3, Brasilia Fernando Cardoso, Brazil's ex-finance minister, has triumphed in his country's presidential election. Cardoso won a majority of votes cast, even though there were seven other candidates. His victory is a sort of thank you from the Brazilian people for the work Cardoso did as finance minister to combat inflation. Once the curse of the Brazilian economy, inflation is now at its lowest for years.

SOCCER STAR TESTS POSITIVE

June 27, Boston, Massachusetts, USA Followers of the USA 1994 Soccer World Cup were today reeling at the news that the Argentinian star Diego Maradona has tested positive for drugs. After his brilliant goal against Greece in an earlier match, it looked as if Maradona's rehabilitation after problems with substance abuse was complete. Now, after an erratic performance against Nigeria two days ago, the footballing career of the man whom many believe to be the finest player the game has ever seen, looks almost certain to be over.

NEW LIGHT ON HUMAN ORIGINS

September 21, Berkeley, California Scientists at the University of California have discovered the fossilised bones of an entirely new species of pre-human. The remains, discovered in Ethiopia, are of an upright creature that walked the Earth 4.4 million years ago. The findings reinforce the idea that apes and humans are both descended from a common ancestor.

1995

KOBE DEVASTATED

January 17, Kobe, Japan Early this morning the Japanese port of Kobe was rocked by a massive earthquake. The death toll is as yet unknown, but Japan's worst quake since 1923 has left at least 250,000 people homeless and caused widespread destruction of buildings, services, roads and railways. Repair and rebuilding will take years and cost billions of yen. Moreover, as Kobe is a key port, the damage to docks and communications will have a serious impact on the country's economy.

Devastation in the wake of the Kobe earthquake.

ROGUE BANKER HELD

March 2, Frankfurt, Germany Following the collapse of the prestigious 233-year-old Barings bank with losses of over $1 billion, German police today arrested 28-year-old British banker Nick Leeson as he was boarding a plane for London. Leeson worked at Barings' Singapore branch, where the gigantic losses occurred. He fled to Germany shortly before the bankruptcy became known. The Singapore authorities have requested that he be returned there to stand trial. Unsupervised by senior staff, Leeson is thought to have traded wildly in the highly risky 'futures' market through a secret account.

HOPES RISE FOR CHECHNYA SETTLEMENT

July 30, Moscow An agreement was signed today between the Russian government and the leaders of the Republic of Chechnya. Following months of bitter fighting, today's accord grants Chechnya widespread self-rule, but not total independence. It remains to be seen how hard-line Chechens, many of whom have taken to the mountains as guerrillas, will react to the settlement.

BOMB BLASTS OKLAHOMA CITY

April 19, Oklahoma City, USA America suffered its worst ever terrorist attack today when a gigantic car bomb blew up the Federal Building in Oklahoma City. Over 200 are believed to have been killed, including several children who were playing in the building's second-floor day-care centre. Efforts to reach those trapped in the wreckage are severely hampered by the likelihood of further collapse. Although police have already apprehended a suspect, no group has yet claimed responsibility for the atrocity.

A firefighter cradles a child shattered by the blast in Oklahoma City.

HUTU MASSACRED

April 22, Kibeho, Rwanda Rwanda's racial tension, responsible for hundreds of thousands of deaths over the last year, today spawned another dreadful massacre. Soldiers of the Tutsi-controlled Rwandan Patriotic Army (RPA) made a dawn raid on the Hutu refugee camp at Kibeho. Hundreds of men, women and children were shot. Many hundreds more were trampled to death in the panic. In their defence, the RPA claims the shooting was started by Hutu gunmen.

WORLD CONDEMNS FRENCH NUCLEAR TEST

September 5, Mururoa, South Pacific France ignored international requests for a halt to the testing of nuclear weapons and today exploded a device beneath the Mururoa atoll in the South Pacific. The effects of the gigantic underground nuclear explosion – equivalent to some 20,000 tons of TNT – were picked up many thousands of miles away. Immediately, angry protests poured in from around the world.

AMERICANS AND RUSSIANS LINK UP IN SPACE

June 29, Space The growing friendship between Russia and the USA today spread beyond the Earth to a point some 250 miles above it. After months of preparation and a final two-hour space chase, the American space shuttle *Atlantis* neatly docked with the Russian space station *Mir* to form the largest space vehicle ever. The astronauts from the two craft greeted each other warmly and chatted away in English and Russian. Scientists hope the mission's success will mean that there will be further astronautical co-operation between the two nations.

Worth the weight? Russian and US astronauts float together aboard the *Mir* space station.

PALESTINIANS TO TAKE OVER WEST BANK

September 28, Washington DC, USA Israelis and Palestinians took another step towards lasting peace today when an agreement was signed in Washington giving Palestinians the right to self-government on the West Bank of the River Jordan. The region, largely inhabited by Palestinian Arabs, has been under Israeli occupation since the Six Day War of 1966. The latest accord allows for the withdrawal of Israeli troops and the election of a Palestinian council.

SIMPSON NOT GUILTY

October 3, Los Angeles, USA After a televised trial that has kept the nation spellbound for months, American football star O.J. Simpson was today found not guilty of murdering his ex-wife Nicole Brown Simpson and her friend Ronald Goldman. The trial received more media coverage than any other in American history. Simpson's African-American background and the fact that the victims were white led to suspicions among the black population that he had been framed by the police. There were fears that, had he been found guilty, race riots would have swept American cities.

Official: not guilty. OJ Simpson shows his delight as he walks free.

PRIME MINISTER RABIN SHOT DEAD

November 4, Tel Aviv, Israel This evening an ultranationalist law student shot dead Israel's peace-promoting Prime Minister, Yitzhak Rabin. The assassin, Yigal Amir, was motivated by his hatred for Rabin's latest agreement with the Palestinians, signed only a few weeks ago. He said God had told him to kill the prime minister as a punishment for betraying his country. The killing raises serious doubts over whether the peace process – detested by extremists on both sides – will survive.

NEWS IN BRIEF ...

POISON KILLERS STRIKE AGAIN

April 19, Yokohama, Japan Less than a month after a terrorist poison gas attack on the Tokyo subway left 12 dead and over 5,000 injured, the same horrifying tactic has been used again. Phosgene gas was released into a crowded train in Yokohama. It spread swiftly into a main station, leaving over 300 travellers gasping for breath. Police suspicions are focused on the fanatical Aum religious cult; some members have been arrested.

Dazed and gasping for breath, Japanese subway passengers recover in the fresh air.

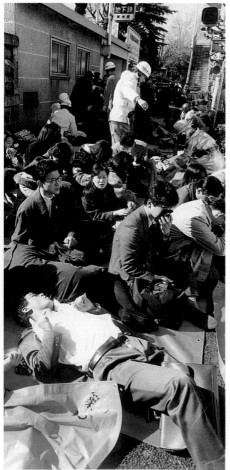

SOCCER STAR KICKS OUT

January 25, London, England The career of the soccer star Eric Cantona hangs in the balance today following a violent incident in yesterday's game between Crystal Palace and Cantona's Manchester United. The referee saw the hot-headed Frenchman kicking Palace defender Richard Shaw and ordered him from the pitch. Approaching the touchline, Cantona was incensed by violent language from a Palace supporter. He vaulted the barrier and assailed his abuser with a kung-fu style kick before officials escorted him away.

TALIBAN ZERO IN ON KABUL

February 14, Kabul, Afghanistan The civil war in Afghanistan has taken an unexpected turn. In under half a year an army of extreme Muslim fundamentalists – the Taliban – has conquered vast areas of the country and is now poised to overwhelm the capital, Kabul. The remarkable success of the Pakistan-trained Taliban, who deny women all political rights, has surprised and shocked most foreign observers.

KEN SARO-WIWA EXECUTED

November 11, Lagos, Nigeria Ken Saro-Wiwa, one of the leading opponents of Nigeria's army dictatorship, was among nine men hanged today for murder. They had been found guilty by a special military court. Saro-Wiwa had long campaigned against the activities of the oil industry, the main source of income for Nigeria's unelected government. His suspect trial and subsequent execution have been widely condemned by the international community.

BOSNIA PEACE HOPE

September 26, Sarajevo, Bosnia There were hopes today that Europe's bloodiest war for fifty years may be over. A peace plan, put together by US statesman Richard Holbrooke, was accepted by representatives of all sides involved in the civil war that has ravaged Bosnia-Herzegovina for much of the 1990s. The power-sharing agreement allows for a united country within which the separate ethnic groups – Croats, Muslims and Serbs – will have their rights enshrined in the constitution. However, there are fears that the settlement may prove too complicated to last.

NORTHERN AUSTRALIANS ACCEPT MERCY KILLING

May 25, Darwin, Australia Adult citizens of sound mind in Australia's Northern Territory have the right, if they are terminally ill and in great pain, to ask that they be put to death. The local legislature today narrowly agreed the measure after hours of heated debate. Mercy killing may be carried out, however, only with the written consent of two doctors, one of whom must be a psychiatrist.

ART WORLD DIVIDED

November 28, London, England The winner of this year's prestigious £20,000 Turner Prize, awarded to a young British artist, has divided the art world. The prize has gone to Damien Hirst, whose principal exhibit – 'Mother and Child, Divided' – consists of half a real cow and half a real calf, preserved alongside each other in separate tanks of formaldehyde. Hirst says his work explores death and isolation. His opponents say it is vulgar sensationalism.

1996

TERRORISTS TARGET LONDON DOCKLANDS

February 10, London Early this evening the Irish terrorist organisation IRA ended its 17-month cease-fire by setting off a massive bomb in east London. The gigantic blast killed two, injured dozens and caused widespread damage to the surrounding buildings. The IRA said it had reluctantly resumed its war with the British government because the British response to its cease-fire had been inadequate.

The bomb had been placed in a lorry parked in an underground car park on the Isle of Dogs, part of the capital's Docklands.

FAIRY TALE'S BITTER END

February 29, London Ending months of rumour, Prince Charles and Diana, Princess of Wales have agreed to divorce. The royal couple are already officially separated, and yesterday's announcement finally brings to a close a tragic tale of broken hearts and promises. Bitterness and misunderstanding remained to the last. The Princess's spokesman said she would keep her royal title and be involved in all decisions about the Princes William and Harry. However, speaking for the Queen, Buckingham Palace said such matters had not yet been discussed.

Royal stand-off: Charles and Diana make their lack of interest in each other plain for all to see.

SENSELESS SLAUGHTER IN SCOTLAND

March 13, Dunblane, Scotland The small Scottish town of Dunblane is tonight in deep mourning. Early this morning a local gun club member, Thomas Hamilton, entered the gym of Dunblane Primary School armed with four loaded handguns. He then proceeded systematically to shoot dead 16 five- and six-year-olds and their teacher, before taking his own life. Twelve wounded children lay among the corpses of their classmates. There seemed to be no motive for the slaughter, and there are already calls for Britain to impose much tighter gun controls.

CLINTON TRIUMPHS IN LOW POLL

November 5, Washington DC Democrat President Bill Clinton has been re-elected to lead the United States of America for another four years. He captured 49% of the vote, with 41% going to his rival, the Republican Bob Dole. Commentators are alarmed, however, by the fact that less than half of all Americans eligible to vote bothered to do so. Clinton's second term in office looks as if it will not be an easy one. The Republican party controls the Senate and the House of Representatives, and the president will have to face ongoing enquiries into his activities when governor of Arkansas.

ISRAELI GUNS POUND UN BASE

April 18, Qana, Lebanon A few days ago, Israel responded to Hezbollah rocket attacks across the Israel–Lebanon border by launching Operation Grapes of Wrath against the terrorist group's bases in southern Lebanon. Today the operation went tragically wrong when Israeli artillery mistakenly targeted a United Nations refugee camp at Qana. More than 100 innocent civilians were killed and hundreds more injured. Although the massacre reflects badly on Israel, Prime Minister Shimon Peres is reluctant to call off the offensive. Tough action, he believes, will force the Lebanese government to take action itself against Hezbollah.

METEORITE FROM RED PLANET DIVIDES SCIENTISTS

August 6, NASA, USA Twelve years after it was discovered in Antarctica, a 1.9-kg meteorite has divided America's scientific community. It is now certain that the meteorite came from Mars, the mysterious 'red planet'. It has long been thought possible that, at one time, Mars hosted some form of life. Daniel Goldin, head of NASA, has fuelled this speculation by announcing that the Antarctic meteorite may hold evidence of microscopic bacterial life on Mars several billion years ago. Other, more sceptical bacteriologists dismiss this speculation as mere wishful thinking.

NEWS IN BRIEF ...

EARTH HEATING UP

January 4, London Early evidence released today suggests that global warming is a reality. According to the British Meteorological Office, which has been compiling weather statistics since 1856, the Earth's average temperature for 1995 was 14.8°C the highest figure on record. It prompted environmentalists to demand immediate cuts in the emission of 'greenhouse' gases.

TURKEY GAGS DISSENT

March 7, Istanbul, Turkey A leading Turkish writer, Yasar Kamal, was today handed down a 20-month suspended gaol sentence for breaking the country's anti-terrorist laws. The court said he had stirred up trouble between Turkey's different racial groups. In fact, he had only criticised the government's curbs on freedom of speech. Turkey's record on human rights is one reason why the European Union has not welcomed it as a member.

EUROPE BANS MAD COW BEEF

March 27, Brussels, Belgium The Veterinary Committee of the European Union today placed a worldwide ban on the export of British beef. The move follows evidence that products from cattle infected with BSE (the so-called 'mad cow disease') can produce a similar fatal disease in humans. Over the past 10 years more than 150,000 cases of BSE have been diagnosed in British cattle.

GORILLA RESCUES CHILD

August 16, Chicago, USA Spectators cried out in horror today when a three-year-old boy accidentally fell 5 metres into the gorilla pit of Chicago's Brookfield Zoo. Their screams soon turned to gasps of astonishment, however, when Binti Jua, a fully-grown female gorilla, loped over to the injured lad, gently picked him up and carried him to an entrance where he could be rescued. Binti Jua's act of unusual tenderness has baffled her keepers.

ELLA FITZGERALD DIES

June 15, Beverly Hills, California, USA The singer Ella Fitzgerald, whose records sold more than 40 million copies, died today at her Californian home aged 79. Her clear voice and wonderful feel for music made her one of the century's most popular artistes. She sang both jazz and ballads, recording many of the works of such master song writers as George Gershwin and Cole Porter.

TOY STORY GOES ON

December 19, London, England A desperate father yesterday paid three times the retail value (£94.00) for a model of Buzz Lightyear, the spaceman hero of the box office hit *Toy Story*. Since its release, the video of the world's first fully computer-animated movie has sold in its millions. Shops have sold out of the plastic model of the Disney character (this year's no.1 Christmas present), and yesterday's extraordinary purchase was made at auction.

JET DOWNS IN ATLANTIC

July 17, New York Mystery surrounds the crash today of TWA flight 800. Shortly after leaving New York, the Boeing 747 burst into flames and plunged into the Atlantic. None of the 230 passengers and crew survived. Those who saw the incident say two explosions rocked the plane before it plummeted into the sea. This has fuelled suspicion that it was either hit by a missile or disabled by an on-board bomb.

1997

Feb 23   Dolly the Sheep cloned
Sept 6   Princess Diana laid to rest
Nov 17   Major Japanese bank crashes
Dec 11   Agreement to curb global
           warming

ADULT MAMMAL CLONED FOR FIRST TIME

February 23, Edinburgh, Scotland Speaking on behalf of a group of researchers working at Scotland's Roslin Institute, Ian Wilmut announced today that his team had successfully cloned an adult sheep. The result, Dolly the sheep, was the first adult mammal ever to be produced by such methods. Dolly was grown from DNA in the womb of a host 'mother' ewe. The success of the experiment raises a host of ethical difficulties. If a sheep can be cloned, for example, then it ought to be possible to clone any creature. Even a human being.

NEW LABOUR'S NEW START

May 2, London Yesterday the British people voted overwhelmingly to reject the Conservative government, which had been in power since 1979, and turn instead to 'New Labour'. Labour's victory, which gave them a majority of 177 in the 650-seat House of Commons, was their largest ever. Their leader, Tony Blair, is Britain's youngest Prime Minister for 200 years. His remarkable triumph was due partly to Conservative unpopularity and divisions, and partly to Labour's success in swapping its old-fashioned socialist image for one of a modern party wedded to both efficiency and welfare.

WORLD MOURNS ITS 'QUEEN OF HEARTS'

September 7, London Yesterday's funeral of Diana, Princess of Wales, was accompanied by scenes of public grief never before seen in modern times. A million mourners, many in tears, lined the flower-strewn streets of the capital through which her coffin was taken. Half the world followed the funeral service in Westminster Abbey on TV or on the radio. Diana, the self-styled 'Queen of Hearts', had been killed in a high-speed car accident in Paris a week earlier. Her beauty, turbulent private life and high-profile support of many charitable causes had made her one of the most famous people of her generation. Her sudden and tragic death created a vacuum in the lives of millions of people throughout the world.

Princes William (second from left) and Harry (second from right) in mourning at the funeral of their mother, Diana, Princess of Wales.

HOT DEBATE OVER GLOBAL WARMING

December 11, Kyoto, Japan This year's exceptionally powerful El Niño current, producing a Pacific-wide drought and a wave of devastating fires, has raised global warming to the very top of the international agenda. But as we saw during the recent UN Convention on Climate Change, held in Kyoto, Japan, a world-wide consensus on how to tackle the crisis is still far off. Today's Kyoto Protocol calls for reduced emission of climate-altering 'greenhouse' gases, but leaves the details open. Swift and significant cuts would ruin the economies of the major polluters, led by the USA. Tragically, the Earth will probably get much hotter before we take meaningful action – and by then it may well be too late.

TALIBAN TAKE KABUL

September 27, Kabul, Afghanistan Kabul, the capital of Afghanistan, is now in the hands of the Taliban Muslim fundamentalists. Taliban forces, comprised of mainly fanatical young men, have now conquered almost the whole mountainous country. Their leaders crowned one of the most remarkable military campaigns of the decade by declaring Afghanistan to be 'totally Islamic'. This will involve severe religious censorship, strict Koranic justice, and an almost complete loss of rights for women.

TIGERS LOSE THEIR BITE

November 17, Tokyo The so-called 'tiger' economies of Eastern Asia, for 30 years the envy of less dynamic Western countries, are slipping into deep recession. This was confirmed today when the Hokkaido Takushoko Bank, the 10th largest in Japan, announced that it could not meet its debts and would close. The news follows a year of Asian economic woe. In January the South Korean economy began to totter; in August the International Monetary Fund stepped in with a multi-billion-dollar rescue package for Thailand. Indonesia, Hong Kong, Taiwan and other states in the region have all experienced their first economic downturn for a generation.

ALGERIA'S ANGUISH CONTINUES

December 25, Algeria The campaign of merciless murder being waged by Algeria's Muslim fundamentalists has reached new heights of cruelty. Today 27 innocent citizens were massacred in the town of Zouabria. Yesterday the terrorists slaughtered 59 civilians, some in the capital Algiers. On December 23 some 80 men, women and children were brutally slain in the villages of Shari and Sidi al-Antar. The killings are intended to terrorise the population into helping overthrow the government and establish a non-democratic Islamic regime.

NEWS IN BRIEF ...

DENG DIES

February 19, Beijing, China Deng Xioaping, one of the 20th century's most influential figures, died today in Beijing at the age of 92. A keen communist in his youth, in recent years Deng had been responsible for easing China away from the extreme communist policies that had so hampered her economic development. His blend of communist politics with limited free-enterprise has led to spectacular development since the mid-1970s.

HONG KONG REVERTS TO CHINA

July 1, Hong Kong A long chapter in British imperial history ended at midnight when Governor Chris Patten and Prince Charles handed the colony of Hong Kong back to China. Acquired by gunboat diplomacy in 1842, Hong Kong flourished under British rule to become one of the wealthiest regions in Asia. Although China hopes to maintain the territory's prosperity as a 'special administrative region', the civil and political rights currently enjoyed by its citizens are unlikely to last long.

MOTHER TERESA DIES

September 6, Calcutta, India The death was announced yesterday of 87-year-old Gonxha Agnes Bojaxhiu, better known simply as 'Mother Teresa'. The saintly Roman Catholic nun was one of the century's most inspiring figures. Having trained as a nurse in 1948, she founded the Missionaries of Charity and devoted the rest of her life to the poor and outcast of India. She was deeply admired by almost everyone who met her, from Margaret Thatcher to the Cuban communist leader Fidel Castro.

TYSON DISQUALIFIED FOR BITING

June 28, Las Vegas, USA In one of the most extraordinary world championship boxing matches of all time, the challenger Mike Tyson was disqualified for biting the ear of champion Evander Holyfield. Tyson was warned in the third round for chewing a chunk out of Holyfield's right ear. When the fight was restarted and Tyson sank his teeth in the right ear, referee Lane Mills stopped the contest.

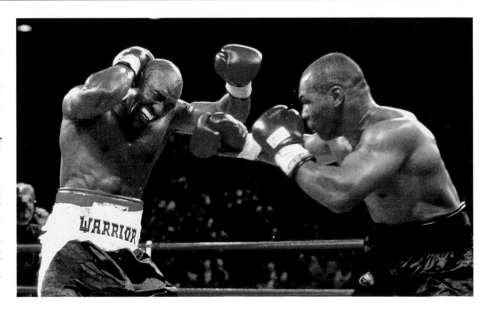

1998

DEVASTATING ICE STORM SWEEPS CANADA

January 11, Quebec, Canada Canada is experiencing what may well prove to be its worst ever national disaster. The recent 5-day ice storm over much of the east of the country has brought down trees, transmission masts and power cables, leaving some 4 million people without power. Schools have been closed and looting has been reported in some blacked-out city centres. So far at least 20 people are said to have died as a result of the freeze. The bill for the damage is estimated at a staggering $2 billion.

TRIAL BY INTERNET FOR PRESIDENT CLINTON

September 11, Washington DC Special Prosecutor Kenneth Starr today published on the Internet his report into the misdoings of US president Bill Clinton. The huge 445-page document describes in detail the relationship between the president and Monica Lewinsky, a former assistant at the White House. Both had previously denied their close relationship. Opinion is divided over the findings. Some Americans say the president should be impeached for perjury. Others, who are perhaps in the majority, believe Clinton's private failings do not undermine his success as president.

The president and the assistant whose revelations threaten his presidency.

SERBS CAPTURE KEY FORTRESS

August 16, Junik, Kosovo, Yugoslavia Serbian forces today tightened their grip over the breakaway province of Kosovo when they captured the key fortress of Junik. Fighting between the Serbs and Kosovo's largely Albanian population has been going on since 1990, when the former Yugoslavia began to break up. The Serbs have been accused of mass destruction of villages and slaughter of their inhabitants to break the resistance of the Kosovo Liberation Army (KLA). Today's news will almost certainly prompt the United Nations into fresh calls for a cease-fire, backed by threats of force if the Serbs fail to comply.

'HAND OF HISTORY' HOPE FOR NORTHERN IRELAND

April 10, Belfast, Northern Ireland More than 17 hours after the passing of the midnight deadline, the parties involved in the Northern Ireland peace talks have finally reached agreement. Prime Minister Tony Blair, who played a key role in the discussions, said he had 'felt the hand of history' had been upon the negotiators. The agreement envisages setting up an elected Northern Ireland assembly and establishing new links between the province and the Irish Republic.

LAND-FOR-PEACE DEAL STRUCK OVER WEST BANK

October 23, Maryland, USA It looks today as if a peace deal over the Israeli-occupied West Bank of the River Jordan has finally been hammered out. US President Bill Clinton mediated in the marathon 21-hour bargaining session. Israeli Prime Minister Benjamin Netanyahu has agreed to hand over 13.1 per cent of the West Bank (with 3 per cent as a nature reserve) to the Palestinians. In return, Palestinian President Yasser Arafat will guarantee Israel's security and ensure that the West Bank is not used as a platform for Arab terrorist attacks on Israel.

HONDURAS BEGS FOR HELP

November 2, Managua, Nicaragua Honduran President Carlos Flores today begged the world to help the Central American countries devastated by Hurricane Mitch. In Nicaragua, Honduras, El Salvador and Guatemala, thousands have been killed in villages swept away by floods or buried in mudslides. Crops have been ruined, roads and bridges destroyed, and buildings flattened. Survivors, without shelter, food or fresh water, are threatened by large-scale epidemics of cholera and dysentery.

IRISH PEACE HOPES BLASTED

August 16, Omagh, Northern Ireland The hopes of a lasting peace for Northern Ireland received a terrible setback yesterday when a massive car bomb shattered the town centre of Omagh. The 500lb device exploded in the town's crowded Market Street, killing 28 innocent civilians and injuring over 100 more. A group calling itself the 'real IRA' claimed responsibility for the attack. The breakaway faction is opposed to the Good Friday peace agreement negotiated earlier in the year.

The victims' identities are masked in this photo, taken instants before the explosion.

DESERT FOX BLASTS SADDAM

December 17, Baghdad, Iraq Almost exactly a month since they had delivered a final warning to President Saddam, last night US President Bill Clinton and British Prime Minister Tony Blair ordered massive air strikes against military and illegal weapon-making installations in Iraq. The attacks, code named Operation Desert Fox, saw the night sky over Baghdad lit with tracer and repeated explosions. The sudden move follows Saddam's refusal to re-admit a United Nations weapons inspection team into his country.

NEWS IN BRIEF ...

'UNKNOWN' CIVIL WAR ENDS

February 20, Dhaka, Bangladesh One of the world's longest running but least known civil wars is at an end. The struggle between Bangladeshi forces and warriors of the Buddhist Chakma tribe of the Chittagong region had been going on for almost 22 years. The war, which has cost over 20,000 lives, finally ended when the rebels surrendered their weapons to Prime Minister Sheik Hasina in return for greater self-government.

SINATRA LAID TO REST

May 20, Beverly Hills, California Some 400 mourners, including Gregory Peck, Bob Dylan, Liza Minnelli and Mia Farrow, today attended the funeral of one of the century's most successful and best-loved entertainers. Frank Sinatra, popularly known as 'Ol' Blue Eyes', died of a heart attack at the age of 82. He recorded hundreds of songs and starred in almost 60 movies.

BODY OF MASS MURDERER ON DISPLAY

April 17, Sahook, Cambodia The body of Pol Pot, one of the century's bloodiest dictators, was yesterday put on display in the hut where he died of a heart attack. In the late 1970s, as absolute leader of the communist Khmer Rouge, Pol Pot presided over the senseless slaughter of more than a million of his fellow Cambodians. Anyone who might threaten his dream of a peasant Utopia – including those who did so by wearing glasses – was liable to be killed. Since his overthrow in 1979, the secretive Pol Pot (whose real name was Saloth Sar) always protested, 'My conscience is clear'.

FRENCH WORLD CUP VICTORY

July 13, Paris This evening, watched by a worldwide TV audience of over two billion, the host nation France won an unexpectedly easy victory over the much fancied Brazilians to win the soccer World Cup. The 3–0 scoreline confounded all the pundits' predictions and sent the entire French nation wild with delight.

INDONESIA CELEBRATES

May 22, Jakarta, Indonesia Nationwide celebrations swept Indonesia yesterday at the news that President Suharto has resigned after 32 years in power. Following months of protest and rioting, the authoritarian ruler has made way for the more moderate President Habibie. The new leader has pledged himself to a programme of reform. Even so, he faces a tough task. Indonesia's economy is in a parlous condition, and as a long-standing friend of Suharto, Habibie will find it difficult to convince the 200 million Indonesians that he really has something new to offer.

STARS WATCH GRANDAD BLAST OFF

October 29, Cape Canaveral, Florida The 77-year-old Senator John Glenn, who 36 years ago became America's first astronaut, today returned to space aboard the shuttle *Discovery*. A crowd of almost half a million, including President Clinton, Tom Hanks, Leonardo Di Caprio and Steven Spielberg, watched the faultless blastoff.

1999

ONE UNION, ONE CURRENCY

January 1, Brussels, Belgium At midnight a united states of Europe took a step closer to becoming a reality. The European Union is now using a common currency, the Euro. Although Euro notes and coins will not be in common use for a while, businesses and banks are already using the new money. Britain is the only major EU member not to embrace the Euro from the start. Tony Blair's government has said it will sign up after the new system has had time to settle in, and then only if the British people approve the Euro in a referendum.

NATO ADMITS SLAUGHTER OF REFUGEES

April 19, Brussels NATO's four-week air war against Serbia received a severe setback today when the allies admitted that last week US warplanes had bombed Kosovan refugees. The pilots believed a convoy of tractors, cars and trucks was a Serb armoured column. Dozens of innocent civilians were killed and many more injured. The air strikes are intended to halt Serbian President Milosovic's ruthless 'ethnic cleansing' of Kosovo, which has forced hundreds of thousands of Kosovans – perhaps three-quarters of the province's population – to flee their homes and seek shelter in neighbouring countries. Although NATO has inflicted massive damage on Milosovic's war machine, the ethnic cleansing continues. Today's news is bound to cast doubts on NATO's ability to achieve its aim without sending in ground troops.

PRESIDENT CLINTON CLEARED

February 12, Washington DC, USA The US Senate yesterday failed to find the 2/3 majority needed to impeach President Bill Clinton. He was therefore cleared of the two charges brought against him by the Republican majority in the House of Representatives. So ended only the second impeachment trial in America's 223-year history. Clinton had been accused of lying and trying to cover up his affair with the former White House assistant, Monica Lewinsky. The year-long scandal first enthralled and then bored the American public. Gradually, they became fed up with the Republican Party's witch hunt and swung round in support of their president. In the long run, however, the whole business will probably have done no more than confirm the American people's deep mistrust of all politicians.

RUSSIAN BOMBERS BLAST CHECHENS

September 19, Moscow Russian bombers yesterday pounded guerrilla bases in Chechnya, causing many casualties. At the same time, large numbers of Russian ground troops are reported to be moving cautiously into the troubled Islamic province that is seeking independence from Moscow. The moves, which clearly herald a massive Russian onslaught, follow repeated bomb attacks on Russian cities that have left almost 300 dead. The new prime minister, Vladimir Putin, a former KGB agent, backs the offensive, believing the military action has widespread popular backing and, if successful, will earn votes in Russia's upcoming parliamentary elections.

UN PEACEKEEPERS REACH EAST TIMOR

September 20, East Timor The first troops of the United Nations multi-national peacekeeping force today landed on East Timor, pledged to restore law and order to the strife-torn Southeast Asian state. Since the East Timorese voted overwhelmingly for independence from Indonesia three weeks ago in a UN-sponsored referendum, their country has been terrorised by pro-Indonesian militia. The 20-nation UN force, led by Australian Major General Peter Cosgrove, faces the double task of driving out terrorists while bringing humanitarian aid to the many East Timorese who have fled their homes. Even as the UN troops stepped ashore, smoke billowed from plundered buildings in the East Timorese capital, Dili.

ULSTER GOES IT ALONE

December 2, Belfast, Northern Ireland Today, after 25 years of direct rule from Westminster, London, Northern Ireland begins to rule itself again. The momentous move follows years of on-off negotiation to end the bloody Loyalist (or Protestant) v Republican (or Catholic) 'troubles' that have torn the province apart for so long. Protestant First Minister David Trimble now heads a coalition cabinet that includes Catholic Seamus Mallon as Deputy First Minister. Many pitfalls remain, particularly as paramilitary groups are still armed. But decommissioning is at least being discussed, bringing real hope that Ulster's nightmare is finally over.

WHOLE WORLD GOES PARTYING

December 31–January 1 2000, Auckland, Beijing, Bethlehem, Rome, Paris, Cape Town, London, New York ... To an unknowing alien watching from outer space it must have looked as if the Earth had gone mad. Billions of people in cities, towns and villages around the world welcomed in the year 2000 with the first ever truly international party. The multi-billion-dollar festivities, featuring prayers, bells, sirens, laser shows, fireworks, cheers, toasts, singing and dancing, lasted a full 24 hours as clocks around the circling globe moved inexorably towards the new millennium. Happily, even the feared 'millennium bug' – world-wide chaos when computers failed to recognise the new date – joined in the party spirit and failed to strike.

NEWS IN BRIEF ...

AIDS LINK TO CHIMPANZEES

January 31, London, England Scientists in Britain and America today came up with a new theory about how the AIDS epidemic began. Samples of an AIDS virus found in the blood of African chimpanzees are almost identical to those found in humans, they claim. It is possible, therefore, that the disease crossed the species barrier by people eating meat from infected chimps. The next task is to discover why the virus, which destroys our immune system, leaves chimpanzees unharmed. When that is known, we may learn how to prevent AIDS in humans.

CRIME WAVE THREATENS MANDELA'S FINAL YEAR

February 5, Cape Town, South Africa In his address at the opening of parliament, President Nelson Mandela yesterday promised more resources to combat the tidal wave of crime that is threatening to overwhelm his country. Murders are now happening at the rate of two every minute. Rape, robbery, car hijacks and other violent crimes are soaring. In the cities many South Africans are afraid to leave their homes at night. Mandela is now in his final year as the first democratically elected president of South Africa. He faces the tragic prospect of seeing his presidency, which started with such high hopes, ending in chaos and lawless despair.

KING HUSSEIN DIES

February 7, Aman, Jordan King Hussein of Jordan died today of cancer in an Aman hospital. The 63-year-old king came to the throne in 1952, aged just 16. During his long reign, the British-educated monarch won the reputation of being one of the Middle East's foremost statesmen, and a devoted battler for peace. As ruler of an impoverished kingdom with a large Palestinian population surrounded by volatile neighbours, this was no easy task. Although he joined the Arab war against Israel in 1967, in later years he expelled Palestinian terrorists and made peace with the Jewish state.

TEENAGE MAYHEM IN US

April 20, Denver, USA Two teenage gunmen today went on the rampage through Columbine High School, in the suburbs of Denver, Colorado. The adolescent killers, who finally turned their guns on themselves, murdered 15 and wounded a further 23. The massacre is sure to put further pressure on Congress to tighten up the country's notoriously liberal gun laws.

AROUND THE WORLD IN 19 DAYS

March 20, Mauritania, Northwest Africa The world's last great aviation challenge was overcome today when the British-made Breitling Orbiter 3 crossed the finishing line and completed the first ever round-the-world balloon flight. The epic 19-day journey, covering 26,602 miles at an altitude of around 35,000 feet, was made by British grandfather Brian Jones and his Swiss co-pilot, Bertrand Piccard. Their reward is a $1 million prize and an assured place in aviation history.

GIANT EARTHQUAKE ROCKS TURKEY

August 18, Istanbul, Turkey One of the most powerful earthquakes on record has devastated large areas of western Turkey. Measuring 7.4 on the Richter scale, it is centred around the industrial town of Izmit, some 75 miles from Istanbul. Concrete blocks of flats collapsed like houses of cards, killing thousands while they slept and trapping many more in the rubble. Water and power supplies are broken and there is a serious threat of epidemics.

PEOPLE OF THE NINETIES

Bill Clinton (b. 1946)

President of the United States. A trained lawyer, in 1978 Clinton was elected governor of Arkansas. In 1992, assisted by his sharp mind, youth, good looks and gifts as an orator, he won the Democratic nomination and was elected president. He handled the economy well and used US force wisely abroad in various peacekeeping roles. Re-elected in 1996, his second term was marred by personal scandals of a financial and sexual nature.

Bill Gates (b. 1955)

Computer programmer and businessman. In 1975, William Henry Gates III dropped out of Harvard University to found Microsoft with his friend Paul G. Allen. Their MS-DOS operating system was used by IBM and employed in most personal computers around the world. Microsoft software followed, making Gates a billionaire by the age of 31. By the end of the 90s he was one of the richest and most powerful men in America.

Rupert Murdoch (b. 1931)

Newspaper publisher and media businessman. Australian-born Rupert Keith Murdoch inherited his father's Adelaide newspapers in 1954 and greatly increased their sales with saucy stories of sex and scandal. In the 1960s and 70s he applied the same successful formula to titles he acquired in Britain and America. By the 90s, Murdoch's News Corporation controlled a world-wide empire of newspapers, book publishers, film studios and TV stations, including Sky and Star TV. Murdoch's extraordinary success made him perhaps the world's most influential businessman.

Michael Jordan (b. 1963)

Professional basketball player. Michael Jordan first hit the headlines in 1982 when he made the winning basket for the University of North Carolina in the national championship. In 1984 and 1992 he led the US team to Olympic gold. As a key member of the Chicago Bulls, the 1.98-metre 'Air Jordan' helped his team win six NBA championships (1991–3 and 1996–8). Americans hailed him as the best-known and highest-paid sporting personality in the world.

Nelson Mandela (b.1918)

President of South Africa. Mandela was arrested in 1964 and sentenced to life imprisonment for supporting the armed struggle against South Africa's white apartheid regime. Widespread campaigning led to his release in 1990. As leader of the African National Congress, Mandela steered South Africa towards true democracy and was elected president in 1994. When his term of office ended in 1999 he was recognised as a statesman of the first rank.

Stephen Spielberg (b. 1947)

Film director and producer. After working in TV, in his mid-20s Spielberg moved to full length feature films, making the smash hit *Jaws* in 1975. A string of successes followed, including *Raiders of the Lost Ark* (1981), *ET* (1982), *Schindler's List* and *Jurassic Park* (both 1993), and *Saving Private Ryan* (1998). Spielberg's work won him many awards and made him by far the most popular and successful movie-maker of the 90s.

Princess Diana (1961-97)

Princess of Wales. Diana, the great tragic hero of the decade, stepped into the limelight when she married Prince Charles in 1981. The couple divorced in 1996. Meanwhile, her beauty and charm had made her the darling of the world's media. She overcame personal difficulties and worked tirelessly for many charities before dying in a car crash in Paris.

Oprah Winfrey (b. 1954)

Talk show hostess and actress. Gifted with looks, intelligence and ambition, in 1977 Oprah Winfrey moved from news reporting to hosting a talk show in Baltimore, Maryland. She proved the ideal host – feisty yet fair – and by the 90s her *Oprah Winfrey Show* was recognised as the best of its type in America. She proved an able actress too, and in 1986 was nominated for an Oscar for her role in *The Color Purple*.

Madeleine Albright (b. 1937)

Diplomat and politician. Madeleine Albright's Czech–Jewish family emigrated to the USA in 1948. She worked for the Democratic Party and as a university professor before becoming US ambassador to the United Nations (1993). In 1997 President Bill Clinton made her his secretary of state. In this role she worked to balance America's interests with the quest for peace in the Middle East and Yugoslavia.

Boris Yeltsin (b. 1931)

President of Russia. Engineer Yeltsin joined the Communist Party in 1961 and rose to prominence as a keen reformer. A supporter of democracy and free-market economics, he was elected President of Russia in 1990. His brave defiance of an attempted coup in 1991 left him supremely popular and powerful. Thereafter, hampered by poor health, he struggled to combat Russia's corruption and deep-rooted economic weaknesses before resigning in 1999.

For the first time ever

1990	USA	First large reflecting telescope (Hubble) in orbit
		First detailed pictures of the surface of Venus, from the Magellan probe
	Japan	Laptop computers developed
	Britain	First surgery on a baby in its mother's womb
	Ireland	Mary Robinson Ireland's first woman president
1991	Pacific	First crossing of the Pacific in a hot air balloon (Richard Branson and Per Lindstrand)
	France	Edith Cresson France's first woman prime minister
	USA	Mount Palomar Observatory announces discovery of a quasar, the most distant object yet seen.
		CD-ROMs on sale
1992	USA	Launch of *Endeavour*, new-style space shuttle
	Britain	Betty Boothroyd the first woman speaker of the House of Commons
1993	Antarctica	Ranulph Fiennes and Michael Stroud make first unsupported crossing of Antarctica on foot
	USA	Proposal for a national 'information highway'
	Hawaii	Four large objects discovered beyond Pluto
1994	Britain & France	Channel Tunnel opens
	USA	Virtual Reality available
		First shopping malls on Internet
	Russia	First known Internet bank robber
	South Africa	Nelson Mandela South Africa's first democratically elected president

1995	Russia	Valeri Poliakov remains on *Mir* space station for a record 439 days
	Britain	First implant of a battery-operated heart
		Microsoft introduces Windows 95
1996	Switzerland	First antiatoms produced
	USA	Marathon runner Josiah Thugwane becomes the first black South African to win an Olympic gold medal
1997	USA	High speed Internet access available via cable modems and satellite
		Pilot programme for 'smart' finance cards with onboard computer chips
		Tiger Woods youngest ever and first black golfer to win the US Masters golf championship
	Britain	First cloning of an adult mammal (a sheep)
1998	USA	US Postal Service introduces electronic postage stamps
1999	Mauritania	Briton Brian Jones and Swiss team mate Bertrand Piccard make the first non-stop balloon flight around the world

New words and expressions

The following new words and expressions came into popular use during the nineties. Do you know what they all mean?

blading	genetic engineering	road rage
browser	grunge	snowboarding
cadillacing	hyperlink	surfing the net
carjacking	jungle	televangelist
chat room	mallrats	the third way
comfort food	netiquette	vertically
ecowarrior	popaganda	challenged
fantabulous	rightsize	website

Glossary

apartheid: System of legalized racism in South Africa. Under apartheid, non-white people did not have the vote and had few civil rights.

coup: Swift and forcible seizure of the government.

cruise missiles: Small medium-range guided missiles of great accuracy, normally launched from an aircraft.

Gaza Strip: Narrow strip of land on the coast of the eastern Mediterranean, inhabited largely by Palestinian Arabs, that was occupied by Israel in 1966. In the 1990s it was gradually returned to Palestinian control.

free market economy: An economy governed by the laws of supply and demand rather than controlled by government policy as under communism and socialism.

genocide: Slaughter or attempted slaughter of an entire race, as took place in Rwanda during the mid-1990s.

greenhouse effect: When the atmosphere is thickened by the discharge of gases such as carbon dioxide, it traps the sun's heat like the glass of a greenhouse.

impeach: Trial and declaration of guilt by a legislature, such as a parliament or the US Congress.

left wing: Inclined towards socialism.

loyalist: In Northern Ireland, loyal to the British crown and so opposed to a united Ireland.

NASA: The US National Aeronautics and Space Administration, responsible for overseeing American space travel and research.

referendum: Popular vote on a single issue.

right wing: Favouring free market economics and a minimum of government control over people's lives.

socialist: Favouring the equal distribution of wealth between rich and poor, and government control of the economy.

UN: United Nations Organisation. Based in New York, the UN is engaged in a wide range of international activities, from peace keeping to famine relief.

West Bank: Land on the west bank of the River Jordan, inhabited largely by Palestinian Arabs, that was occupied by Israel in 1966. In the 1990s it was gradually returned to Palestinian control.

Further Reading

Students can find further information on the nineties from past editions of newspapers and magazines and from several sites on the Internet, for example:

The London Times newspaper's website (www.the-times.co.uk/)

Newsweek's website (www.newsweek.com/)

The New York Times' website (www.nytimes.com)

The Telegraph (www.telegraph.co.uk)

Time Magazine (www.time.com)

Index

Note: References to 'People of the Nineties' are in **bold** type.